FRENCH PASTRY MADE SIMPLE

FOOLPROOF RECIPES FOR ÉCLAIRS, TARTS, MACARONS AND MORE

MOLLY WILKINSON, Creator of MollyJWilk Pastry

PAGE STREET
PUBLISHING CO.

PAGE STREET
PUBLISHING CO.

First published in 2021 by

Page Street Publishing Co.

27 Congress Street, Suite 1511

Salem, MA 01970

www.pagestreetpublishing.com

Distributed by Macmillan, sales in Canada by The Canadian Manda Group.

25   24   23   4   5

ISBN-13: 978-1-64567-217-3

ISBN-10: 1-64567-217-4

Library of Congress Control Number: 2020945293

Cover and book design by Laura Benton for Page Street Publishing Co.

Photography by Joann Pai

Author photo by Claire Emmaline

Printed and bound in the United States

TO MY MOM,

WHO ENCOURAGED AND INSPIRED ME TO BAKE UP
A STORM IN THE KITCHEN FROM A YOUNG AGE

✦ CONTENTS ✦

INTRODUCTION

Would you be surprised if I told you that French pâtisserie could be easy? That all those stunning desserts go back to a few basic French pastry recipes that have been refined and finessed for generations?

This cookbook contains ten foundational French pastry recipes that will help you master over 60 desserts, counting variations! Conquer pâte à choux dough and you'll be whipping up éclairs, cream puffs, Saint-Honoré and more. Learn how to make pastry cream, including different flavor options, and you have a gorgeous custard filling to put inside! All of the recipes are intertwined, so by mastering just ten, you will soon be well on your way to creating your own mini pastry shop at home.

I've combed through modern and historical versions of these foundational recipes, collaborated with chef friends, used my knowledge in the kitchen and extensively tested, making them foolproof for the home baker. Have you ever wondered what speed your mixer should be on when making a meringue? Or what the texture of certain doughs should look like? I provide in-depth explanations of the methods and detailed instructions so you feel like I'm right there with you in the kitchen, guiding you through new techniques with ease.

I have to admit, I'm not one of those strict French pastry chefs. I believe a pastry should taste incredible, be easy to make and allow for your own creativity to shine through! Does an opéra cake have to follow the 3-centimeter French height regulation? Nah. I'd rather all the flavors be balanced in the right quantities than have you wrangle a super-thin piece of cake! I want to build your pastry-making confidence and give you the information you need to succeed whether you're a beginner or seasoned baker.

Little historical pastry stories and tidbits about my life here in France pop up in the book. I moved to Paris in 2013 to follow my passion by studying pâtisserie at Le Cordon Bleu. It was a huge shift from my nine-to-five marketing job, but I quickly fell in love with the pastries, the intoxicating buzz at the farmers' markets and a culture that revolves around good food and good ingredients. This was what I wanted my life to be: sugar, butter and sharing the joy that comes from baking something delicious.

After graduating, I worked in pâtisseries across the United States and in France. I went from châteaux to cooking schools to French farmhouses, soaking up as much information as I could. Today, I live in Versailles with a Frenchman, where I teach small, private, in-person classes and virtual classes to people all over the world. They are about having fun and making French pastry easy and accessible. All the tips I share in my classes, and so much more, have gone into this book to make it an ultimate guide to baking pâtisserie.

I hope this cookbook will soon be covered in smears of chocolate and tons of notes. Bake with confidence, follow your intuition and taste all those cake scraps!

WHAT EVERY HOME PASTRY CHEF NEEDS TO KNOW BEFORE BEGINNING

Pastry certainly does not have to be difficult and can be achieved with very minimal tools in the kitchen. A couple of key pieces of equipment will make it that much easier, and using delicious ingredients will bring the flavor over the top with these fabulous French recipes.

Flip back to this section to stock up on helpful tools, to find tips for piping and using a scale and to refer to a piping tip reference chart when all those codes become a bit confusing.

INGREDIENTS

These recipes are all about accessibility and use commonly found ingredients that you probably already have in your pantry. To make them shine even more, use good-quality ingredients when you can and shop the seasons. For example, make the Strawberry Fraisier (page 41) when strawberries are at their peak. For a splurge, spring for a vanilla bean when baking a cake for a special occasion. For desserts where the main ingredient is chocolate, go for one that's a tad more expensive. Make these little tweaks and you'll be seriously happy with the boost of flavor in the final dessert.

A couple of key points:

- Heavy cream is the same as heavy whipping cream or whipping cream.

- Powdered sugar is the same as confectioners' sugar and icing sugar.

- Ground almonds are sold as meal (almonds with the skins on) or flour (blanched almonds with the skin removed). Almond meal will have little specks in it from the skin. For all recipes in this book, either can be used. For the best visual result for the French Macaron Tower (page 75), however, I would recommend a finely ground almond flour; otherwise, the macarons will appear speckled.

- When looking for the best chocolate, keep an eye out for (in no particular order) Valrhona, Guittard, Ghiradelli, Cacao Barry®, Lindt, Scharffen Berger, Callebaut and other local brands in your area.

- Use fresh egg whites when they'll be whipped up in the recipe, as often carton egg whites do not whip.

- All of the recipes are made to work with all-purpose flour, as it is the most widely available. Take a look, though, as you might find a fabulous local flour mill in your community. You can use finer flours for all recipes except the Pâte à Choux (page 83), where the higher protein and grind of an all-purpose flour is recommended. For the Pâte Sucrée tart crust recipe in particular (page 17), there is a slight adjustment to be made if using a more finely ground pastry or cake flour.

THE ONLY EQUIPMENT YOU NEED

Two of my absolute favorite shops in Paris are E.Dehillerin and Mora, pastry equipment stores chock-full of treasures. E.Dehillerin dates back to 1820 and I don't think it has changed the inside since! It resembles a hardware store, with tart rings hung from the ceiling, cubbyholes of whisks, passageways that veer off in random directions and a gated basement full of massive copper pots and pans. The staff know me there by name now as they jot down the items I want after referring to a hefty catalog to match the code stamped on each with a price. Every purchased item is hand-wrapped in brown paper and secured with the shop's signature yellow and green tape.

A lot of special equipment can go along with making pastry—such as metal cake rings and acetate plastic! Here's the thing, though: Besides having far too many kinds of tart rings to count (I LOVE the variation), my equipment stockpile is more minimal than you'd think. I don't believe in pans that are made for just one cake (the exception being a madeleine pan!) and often when I'm baking on the road, I make do with what is on hand. In that same spirit, I created this book to work with just a few standard pans. This meant some nontraditional uses for some, but I'm really pleased with the results.

PANS AND TINS

CAKE PANS: 8- AND 9-INCH (20- AND 23-CM) ROUND

The pans are used for tracing circles on parchment paper to get certain dimensions, assembling the Tarte Tatin (page 147) in to allow for an easier flip and, *bien sûr,* baking cakes!

SPRINGFORM PAN: 9-INCH (23-CM) ROUND

Besides baking the Vanilla Bean Flan (page 37) inside it, this pan serves a very useful purpose for lots of the fancier cakes in this book, where the outside ring jumps in to fill the purpose of a traditional metal cake ring. Placed on a serving platter, it provides support during assembly for the Charlotte aux Fraises (page 125) and Strawberry Fraisier (page 41). Open up the latch before serving. Remove the strip of parchment paper protecting the cake from sticking to the pan. And reveal rows of ladyfingers and a perfect line of strawberries.

MUFFIN TIN: 12-WELL

I had a lot of fun using this in slightly unconventional ways. Did you know that, in a pinch, madeleines can be baked in a muffin tin? *Mais, oui oui!* The Moelleux au Chocolat (page 59) are baked inside and then carefully flipped out for easier pickup. The Tigré Almond Cakes (page 51) are often made with a special mold. But with a muffin tin and a teaspoon-sized measuring spoon, I've made them look identical to those you find in pâtisseries.

JELLY-ROLL PAN: 10 X 15–INCH (25 X 38–CM)

A bit more specialized as pans go, but still standard. For the Rolled Génoise Cake (see page 105), this is the dimension to use and what the recipes have been configured for. It's handy to use as an extra cookie sheet, too!

TART PAN: 9- TO 9½-INCH (23- TO 24-CM) OR INDIVIDUAL 4-INCH (10-CM) TARTLET

I have a huge love affair with tart pans. I have mini ones in six different designs, rings with straight sides, pans with removable bottoms and ruffled edges, individual squares and circles and one of my all-time favorites, a long rectangle that is always a showstopper!

You certainly don't have to have all of these, but maybe I'll inspire you to create a collection of your own. All the recipes work with either a 9- to 9½-inch (23- to 24-cm) standard tart pan, six 4-inch (10-cm) individual tart pans or the rectangular 4 x 14–inch (10 x 35.5–cm) tart pan too.

BAKING PANS: 9 X 13–INCH (23 X 33–CM) AND 9-INCH (23-CM) SQUARE

These pans are super useful for making the Opéra Cake (page 111), where three rather thin pieces of rectangular cake are needed.

MADELEINE PAN AND RAMEKINS (NONESSENTIAL)

For the signature shell shape, you really can't get around using anything but a madeleine pan. A metal pan is best for getting that signature bump on top and a nice golden brown color. Not to worry if you don't have one, though, as they'll bake up just fine in a muffin tin! The ramekins can be used for Moelleux au Chocolat (page 59) or the Crème Caramel (page 161).

YOUR PASTRY TOOL KIT

BAKING SCALE

THE #1 MOST IMPORTANT TOOL FOR PASTRY

Scales are very easy to use, inexpensive, save on cleanup and make sure your measurements are accurate! Have I convinced you yet? Using a scale takes your baking to the next level, as your measurements are exactly what the recipe writer wants you to use. With cups, though, with each baker and how they dip, scrape and shimmy the ingredient inside, you can see huge variations in the final amount.

The best example is flour. A lot of chefs will instruct how they specifically want you to measure flour with cups for the best result for their recipes. One chef might say spoon the flour into the cup and then level it off with the back of a knife, whereas another chef would suggest sifting the flour first and then delicately putting it into the cup. The beauty of a scale . . . 100 g of flour is always 100 g of flour, no matter what. Just pour it into a bowl with your scale at zero until it reads 100. Easy!

USING A SCALE

When you turn on a scale, it first has to calibrate to zero, just like a scale you use to weigh yourself. You can press On with nothing on the scale, or go ahead and place the bowl you'll be using on top, then press On and wait for it to show "0." Select the type of measurement you want to use (g/kg, ml or lb/oz). Then, pour in what you would like to measure, slowly watching the weight. When you get close to the amount you want, stop every once in a while to allow the scale to catch up. To measure the next ingredient, push the On button, Zero or Tare to bring the number to zero. No math required!

SMALL METAL OFFSET SPATULA

So handy for spreading a filling inside a cake, smoothing the top of Rolled Génoise Cake batter (page 105), icing a Bûche de Noël (page 118) with ganache, and so much more!

ROLLING PIN

My favorite is the French rolling pin, a long straight rod with no handles and no taper so I can feel the amount of pressure I'm applying. Any rolling pin works though, and in a pinch, why not use a wine bottle?

THERMOMETER

For Italian meringue and French buttercream, an instant-read digital thermometer is essential. A probe thermometer is easy, as you can place it in the pot and not have to worry about holding it. A meat thermometer or one you hold will work, too, though.

LARGE AND SMALL SIEVE OR SIFTER

For sifting dry ingredients for cakes or macarons, or ensuring a smooth lemon curd, I prefer a large sieve with a medium-coarse mesh. It's often less frustrating than a very fine mesh. The purpose is to get rid of lumps, not strain out tiny particles as you would for a sauce. *Psst.* I'll only tell you to sieve something when it's absolutely necessary.

I love a small sieve or sifter for a sprinkling of powdered sugar or cocoa powder for a finishing touch.

LEMON SQUEEZER

Essential in my book if I'm making anything that requires freshly squeezed lemon or lime juice!

Pictured from left to right, read about the following tips in the chart below: round 5 mm, round 8 mm, round 10 mm, round 12 mm, open star 11 mm, Saint-Honoré, open star short prongs 11 mm.

FILLING AND WORKING WITH A PIPING BAG

DISPOSABLE PIPING BAGS

One of the most useful tools you can have when making pastry. I have a roll of one hundred 21-inch (53-cm) Matfer bags that I pull from just about every day. Instead of thinking about them just as a means to decorate, think of them as a tool, too. Pâtissiers use them to quickly and evenly distribute fillings and cake batters. They allow more control and easier cleanup. I prefer disposable bags, as often they have a much better grip, can be cut to fit any tip or simply the end can be snipped off to the appropriate length. Ateco has great options with packs of 18-inch (46-cm) and 21-inch (53-cm) bags. I like working with larger-sized bags, as I can always cut the length down if I need to and it means that I can fit all the batter in at once.

PIPING TIPS

Just as with my tart pans, I have amassed a collection of piping tips, but I always go back to the same seven tips over and over again. The easiest to use and what all pastry professionals work with are the large tips, either plastic or metal, that do not require couplers. Because the codes can vary across brands, I've included the millimeter measurement for the openings and the equivalents for both Ateco and Wilton. I prefer Matfer and Ateco as they are geared more for pastry, especially for piping doughs.

PIPING REFERENCE CHART

Size/Type	Size	Ateco	Wilton
Round 5 to 6 mm (to fill choux)	3/16" or just under 1/4"	801 & 802	9 & 10
Round 8 mm (for piping and filling macarons)	5/16"	803	12
Round 10 mm (for piping and filling macarons and small choux)	3/8"	804	2A
Round 12 mm (large choux)	Just under 1/2"	806	1A
Open Star 11 mm (E5 or E6) (for decoration)	7/16"	824 or 825	1M
Saint-Honoré (for decorating)	Sizes vary	880 & 882	N/A
Open Star Short Prongs 11 mm (also called French) (PF16) (for éclairs or decoration)	7/16"	864 or 865	6B

INSERTING A PIPING TIP

Open up the bag and fold back the sides. This gives you something to hold on to while filling the bag and keeps it clean. Place the tip inside and press down, stretching the bag around the end of the tip to make sure it's secure.

To cut off the end of a disposable bag, use a pair of scissors to apply pressure (as if you were cutting the tip) at the halfway point on the tip. Move the scissors around the tip in a circle, to score and cut the plastic. Pull off the end (you might need to apply a little force, depending on the cut)!

APPLYING A LOCK

To make sure runny batter doesn't flow out the end, twist the bag once right above where the tip is and press the twisted part snuggly into the tip. To remove, simply pull out and untwist.

FILLING A PASTRY BAG

Cup your hand in a C shape and place it inside the folded back section of the bag, right at the crease. Take a big scoop of the mixture with your other hand and put it inside. Scrape the spatula on your hand that is holding the bag. Only fill your bag halfway full, for the most amount of control.

PIPING

There are lots of ways to hold a piping bag. The most important is to find what is comfortable for you! Always twist the top of the bag to keep what's inside secure. You can then press from the top with one hand and guide the tip with the other or, as I do when working with large piping bags, cut off the batter about one-quarter of the way up the bag from the tip. I hold my hand in an "okay" position, my thumb and first finger connecting to confine part of the batter to a small reservoir. I press with my other three fingers to push the batter through the tip. When I run out of batter in my "reservoir," I open up the "okay" fingers and press more through, using my hand that's at the top of the bag to push it down.

NONESSENTIAL BUT HANDY TOOLS TO COMPLETE YOUR KIT

SILICONE BAKING MATS

These are fantastic when you need a nonstick baking surface and economical, too. They are ideal for macarons, as they help them keep their round shape. I often use them interchangeably with parchment paper to line baking sheets. I prefer Silpat® brand mats.

PLASTIC SCRAPER

This almost made it into the essentials, but it's really only used for two doughs: pâte sucrée and pâte feuilletée. This makes it so easy to scrape up the dough when bringing the pâte sucrée together, or to clean up any bits that have stuck to your work surface. They're really inexpensive, too!

PASTRY BRUSH

This is great for applying egg wash or water to doughs. You can also use a crumpled-up paper towel.

TORCH

You can find these at the hardware store or baking shops, or online. Look for one that allows you to adjust the strength of the flame. This is for toasting meringue, such as the top of the Tarte au Citron Meringuée ou Pas! (page 71), but also handy for heating a mixer bowl to warm up butter or icing that's inside.

FLOUR BRUSH

Great for brushing off excess flour when rolling out doughs and for easy cleanup of floury work surfaces, too!

SCOOP

For evenly doling out batter for Moelleux au Chocolat (page 59), Earl Grey Madeleines (page 56) or Tigré Almond Cakes (page 51), this is the best tool to use. It makes it less messy, too! For small cakes, I often use size #16 (¼ cup [60 ml]). For truffles and madeleines, I opt for one that's a little smaller in size, #60 (1 tablespoon [15 ml]).

PÂTE SUCRÉE:
THE ONLY TART
DOUGH YOU NEED

French tarts are all about the perfect crust! In fact, there are many different kinds, all with varying amounts of butter and sugar. Pâte sucrée is my favorite by far. There is the addition of almond flour, vanilla and powdered sugar to the dough, making it much more than just a base to hold fillings. It melts in your mouth, but is crisp at the same time.

Roll it out on its own to form a stand-alone Rustic Seasonal Fruit Galette (page 23), no tart pan needed! Cut out cookies to slather with jam and stack to make Lunettes de Romans (page 29).

Get ready to make this your go-to tart crust. It's just waiting to be filled with chocolate ganache (page 51), pastry cream and berries (page 44), Lemon Curd (page 67) and so much more!

BASE RECIPE: PÂTE SUCRÉE

MAKES ENOUGH FOR TWO 9- TO 9½-INCH (23- TO 24-CM) TART SHELLS OR TWELVE 4-INCH (10-CM) ❧ INDIVIDUAL TART SHELLS ❧

This, for me, is the ultimate tart dough. It's so much more than just butter and flour and tastes utterly divine! It's crisp with a texture similar to that of a shortbread cookie. Pâte sucrée is very different from a pie dough (pâte brisée) or puff pastry (pâte feuilletée, page 139), where water brings together flour and big pieces of butter to form a beautiful flaky dough. Instead, the butter is thoroughly worked in and barely any water is used, so the resulting dough looks and tastes like a cookie batter.

The bonus of this base recipe is that it makes two crusts for the same work as one! This means you can make two tarts now for a fabulous get-together, or freeze the rest for later.

2⅔ cups (340 g) all-purpose flour

1 cup (120 g) powdered sugar

⅓ cup (30 g) almond flour or meal (see Variation)

¼ tsp salt

14 tbsp (1½ sticks + 2 tbsp [200 g]) unsalted butter, cold, cubed

1 large egg

1½ tsp (scant 8 ml) vanilla extract

1 tsp water (see Variation if working with pastry or cake flour)

You can mix the dough together in a stand mixer or by hand.

IN A STAND MIXER

In the bowl of a stand mixer fitted with the paddle attachment, combine the flour, powdered sugar, almond flour, salt and cold cubed butter, and mix them together on low speed until the mixture looks sandy, about 5 minutes.

This is called *sablage*, meaning "sand" in French. Watch carefully as once it reaches this state, you want to stop the mixer so the butter doesn't get warm and form a dough all on its own (see picture 1 on page 16).

In a small bowl, whisk together the egg, vanilla and water and then add to the mixer. Mix on low speed, watching closely, until it comes together as a dough. (see picture 2 on page 16).

As soon as this happens, turn off the mixer to prevent the dough from overmixing and shrinking when baked.

If there are a few crumbly bits left on the bottom of the bowl that didn't mix in, press those into the rest of the dough with a spatula. The dough might be slightly sticky.

(CONTINUED)

TO MIX BY HAND

In a small bowl, whisk together the egg, vanilla and water and set aside.

In a large bowl, combine the flour, powdered sugar, almond flour and salt. Mix together briefly with a whisk or clean hand.

Add the cold cubed butter and toss to coat with the flour mixture.

TIP

If the butter is so cold it's hard to press, it is worth waiting a couple of minutes for it to warm up slightly before moving on.

Incorporate the butter, working it in by hand until it is in small pieces. The motion you'll make is what one of my chef instructors called "show me the money": Scoop up the mixture with both palms facing up, and then press the butter pieces with your thumb moving along slightly open fingertips (see picture 3 on page 16).

This motion smears and presses the butter, breaking it into smaller pieces and mixing it with the dry ingredients.

Work fast. If the butter starts to become too warm and melts, it will form a dough before the liquid is added. The end result won't be the same—so, if needed, place the whole bowl in the refrigerator or freezer for 10 to 15 minutes, to chill the butter before continuing.

Aim for having mostly all small pieces. Several larger pieces are fine as well, as everything will be brought together later.

Pour in the egg mixture and mix in well with a fork or one finger to avoid the rest of your hand getting super messy.

Empty out into a mound on a clean surface. Using the bottom part of your palm (closest to your wrist) and starting at the top of the pile, farthest from you, press and smear the dough forward and away from you in multiple strokes, streaking the mixture across the work surface (this is called *fraisage* [see picture 4 on page 16]).

Once you've worked your way through all of the dough, scrape it together into a pile (a plastic dough scraper is great for this) and start again, repeating until the dough comes together. The amount of times you will have to do this depends on the temperature of your ingredients and kitchen. The dough might be a little sticky.

ONCE THE DOUGH IS FORMED

Divide in half and wrap each piece in plastic wrap. Press flat to form a disk (this helps it cool more quickly and more evenly), and chill in the refrigerator for at least 45 minutes before rolling out and shaping to the mold.

ROLL OUT THE DOUGH

Before starting to roll out your dough, check its temperature. You want it to be cold but pliable (normally, freshly made dough hits this point after chilling in the refrigerator for 45 minutes).

Test this by seeing how much of an indentation you can make in the top with a finger. Press on both the sides and the center to make sure the temperature is even throughout. No indentation means it's far too cold to attempt to roll. A very easy, deep indentation means it's too warm and will be too soft to work with. You're aiming for something in between: cold and firm, but still able to make a fairly easy indentation at all points across the top of the dough.

If your dough is very cold, let it sit on your kitchen countertop for 5 to 10 minutes (or more) before working with it. The amount of time it takes depends on the temperature of your kitchen and the starting temperature of the dough.

The best method for rolling out any dough is to move it frequently on a lightly floured surface. This prevents sticking as the bottom is always coated with flour even as it expands, but also works the dough more evenly. Start gently with the pressure, as being forceful with a cold dough can cause cracks (see picture 1 on page 21). Concentrate the motion in front of you, turning the dough to access different areas. I will make two or three rolls, then pick up the dough and swish it around on my surface, giving it a 90-degree turn to resume rolling a new section of dough. As the dough warms up with the friction of the rolling pin, it will be easier to roll. Add more flour as needed (see picture 2 on page 21).

TIP

Thickness is preferential, but you need enough dough to actually form to your mold. I like it to be around ⅛ inch (3 mm).

CRACKING EXPLAINED

A little bit of cracking around the edges when rolling out is normal and not a big deal. Big cracks, though, can make it difficult to work with. So, how do you avoid them? Yet again, it all goes back to the temperature of the dough. When working with very cold, firm dough, rolling and pressing down forcefully will cause it to crack. If the dough is too warm, it won't hold its shape and can crack.

If your dough has chilled unevenly and is not the same temperature throughout (the middle is soft, but the sides hard), this will cause it to crack as well. The best way to fix this is to simply let it chill for longer in the fridge. You can also massage around the sides to warm it to the same temperature as the middle.

LINE THE TART PAN

There is no need to grease a tart pan as there is so much butter in the crust, it won't stick.

To make sure you have enough dough to fill the mold, place the pan on top of the dough. Ensure you have about a 2-inch (5-cm) margin and then cut away any excess.

For smaller molds: Simply pick up the circle of dough and place it on top of the mold.

For larger molds: Either fold the dough in half, pick it up with both hands, fingers outstretched, place in the mold and unfold; or, if you are rolling out on a nonstick mat or parchment paper, place a hand on top of the rolled-out dough, flip and set it on top of the mold, peeling away the mat or paper.

If it is not easy to remove, your dough is too warm. Don't force it; instead chill the rolled-out dough for 10 minutes and try again.

Bring the dough up with your hands so the middle of the dough is touching the bottom of the pan and the edges are up around the sides of the pan.

Hold the excess dough with your less dominant hand so it is supported, and help it down the sides. Then, with your dominant hand, press the dough into the corners around the edge. I do this with my index finger curled up like a hook—it's the perfect angle (see picture 3 on page 21).

TIP

If the dough cracks or there isn't enough coverage, do a bit of patchwork—absolutely not a problem!

(CONTINUED)

Cut off excess dough by rolling across the top of the mold with a rolling pin (see picture 4 on page 21). Then, pinch around the edges one last time to press the dough back flush against the sides, as an air bubble is created by rolling across the top.

After lining the tart shell(s), prick all over the bottom with a fork (this is called docking). This helps prevent the dough from rising in the middle when baking. Chill completely in the fridge (20 to 30 minutes) or freezer (15 minutes) before baking. If it is well chilled before baking, you don't need to use pie weights or baking beans!

BAKE

To blind bake (bake the shell completely without a filling), preheat your oven to 325°F (165°C) and then bake for 25 to 30 minutes, or until the whole surface is evenly golden brown. If the center of the crust rises during baking, open the oven and gently press it down, using a dry tea towel or oven mitt.

To bake with a filling inside, see the specific recipe instructions.

REMOVE FROM THE TART PAN

If using a pan with a removable bottom, simply press up on the bottom and the tart crust will pop up while the ring will slide down your arm. You can remove the pan's base or leave it on. For small tartlet pans without a removable bottom, place a hand on top and flip for the tart crust to slide out. If the tart crust is stuck, look for where the crust is over the sides of the mold attaching itself to the pan. Loosen this carefully with a knife and then try again.

MAKE AHEAD

The tart dough can be made 3 days in advance and kept in the fridge. Store in the freezer for 1 month, wrapped tightly in plastic wrap and placed in a freezer bag. Thaw at room temperature for 20 to 30 minutes or overnight in the fridge.

VARIATION

To make the crust chocolate: Replace ¼ cup (30 g) of the flour with unsweetened cocoa powder.

Use a food processor: To make the dough, follow the instructions for the stand mixer, blitzing in the butter in several bursts.

Make it nut-free: The almond flour can be replaced with all-purpose flour.

For finer flours: This recipe was designed to work with all-purpose flour, as it is the most accessible. Finer pastry or cake flours are wonderful for this dough as well. If using finer flours, keep the flour quantity the same, but omit the teaspoon of water, as the extra liquid won't be needed.

No stress: If you are having trouble rolling out and lining the tart pan, simply press the dough in, using the flat bottom of a cup.

RUSTIC SEASONAL FRUIT GALETTE

❧ SERVES 4 TO 6 ❧

The perfect tart to make at a moment's notice. No tart mold is needed; it's striking in appearance and minimal effort is involved. For the filling, play around with whatever fruit is in season. Think crisp apples, pears and figs in the fall and peaches, berries and nectarines in the summer! You can make this tart with just one fruit, or mix it up with a combination. For the pictured fruit galette, I used two sliced peaches and a 4-ounce (125-g) container each of blueberries and raspberries.

The key to a successful fruit galette lies in the juiciness (water content) of the fruit. Too much juice from ripe fruit and the tart bottom could get soggy. Keep your very soft fruits for pies—or the sheer joy of eating them over a sink—and use your less ripe fruits for this tart. I've also built in a little "insurance policy" to help keep the bottom nice and crisp. The almond flour can be omitted, if necessary, but I love the cakelike texture it creates when it mixes with the fruit juices.

This is great served with a dollop of sweetened whipped cream or still warm from the oven with a big scoop of ice cream!

½ recipe Pâte Sucrée (page 17)

3 cups (500 g) fresh or frozen fruit, or a combination of both

1 tbsp (8 g) all-purpose flour, plus more for dusting

1 tbsp (15 g) granulated sugar

Optional additions: zest of a citrus fruit, a handful of dried or fresh cranberries, ½ tsp of ground spices such as cinnamon, ginger or nutmeg

1 tbsp (6 g) almond flour or meal (optional)

A splash of milk

1 tbsp (15 g) raw or granulated sugar

Sliced raw almonds (optional)

Start by making the pâte sucrée.

While the tart dough chills, prepare your fruit: For stone fruits, apples or pears, slice into ½-inch (1.3-cm) pieces, skin on or off. Hull strawberries; large ones should be quartered or halved. For figs, quarter or halve, cutting off the stem. Pit cherries. Berries, such as raspberries, blueberries and blackberries, are good to go!

Place the fruit in a large bowl.

In a separate bowl, whisk together the all-purpose flour, granulated sugar and your choice of optional add-ins (if using). Sprinkle over the fruit and toss to coat. Let sit at room temperature while you prepare the crust.

Roll out the tart dough in a big circle on a lightly floured surface to about ⅛ inch (3 mm) thick and 11 to 12 inches (28 to 30 cm) in diameter. Transfer to a baking sheet lined with either parchment paper or a silicone baking mat.

TIP
You can roll out the dough on parchment or a baking mat, then simply pick up the whole lot and place on the baking sheet.

(CONTINUED)

Sprinkle the almond flour in a circle in the middle of the tart dough. This will help absorb some of the juices from the fruit and form a thin, almost cakelike layer at the bottom.

Pile the fruit in the center and spread out on the dough in a circle, aiming for an even layer about an inch (2.5 cm) high. Allow for about a 2-inch (5-cm) margin. Arrange the topmost fruit pieces however you'd like them for the final presentation.

Fold the edges of the dough up and over the fruit, making rough pleats. You can use the parchment paper or baking mat to help lift and press the dough around the sides. Lightly brush the dough with milk, then sprinkle the whole top (including the fruit) with the raw sugar. If using, scatter sliced almonds on the crust and a bit of the fruit.

Chill for 30 minutes. Meanwhile, preheat your oven to 375°F (190°C). It's helpful to use convection for this, if you have it. No need to change the baking temperature.

Bake for 30 to 35 minutes, or until the crust is evenly golden brown and the filling is bubbling.

Remove from the oven and allow to cool on the baking sheet for 1 to 2 hours, to let the filling set. Serve warm or at room temperature.

STORAGE
Best the day it's made, but fabulous the next two days as well (especially for breakfast). Keep chilled in the fridge.

MAKE AHEAD
Prepare the pâte sucrée in advance.

NOTE
This tart can be assembled in a parchment-lined pie dish as well.

CHOCOLATE-WALNUT-PEAR TART WITH CARAMEL SAUCE

 SERVES 6 TO 8

Pears, walnuts and chocolate drizzled with caramel sauce make for a gorgeous flavor combination. This recipe is great for getting creative with the design of the pears on top and little spice additions to the caramel. Maybe add a bit of cinnamon? Make this recipe even easier by replacing the caramel sauce with big scoops of ice cream or omitting it completely. For the pear decoration, I've included several ideas from no-fuss to more design-oriented, so have fun with it—it will be delicious, no matter what.

½ recipe chocolate Pâte Sucrée (page 17)

CHOCOLATE-WALNUT CAKE

½ cup (60 g) walnut halves or pieces

2 oz (60 g) bittersweet or semisweet chocolate (60 to 70%)

¼ cup (4 tbsp [60 g]) unsalted butter, cubed, at room temperature

½ cup (60 g) powdered sugar

1 tsp all-purpose flour

Pinch of salt

1 large egg

TO ASSEMBLE

3 to 4 firm Anjou pears (see Notes)

1 tbsp (15 ml) melted unsalted butter

WALNUT-CARAMEL SAUCE

1 recipe Molly's Favorite Salted Caramel Sauce (page 159)

½ cup (60 g) walnut halves, chopped

Optional: ½ tsp ground cinnamon, ginger or cardamom

Make the pâte sucrée first if you haven't done so in advance, so it has time to chill while you prepare the rest of the recipe.

PREPARE THE CHOCOLATE-WALNUT CAKE BATTER

Pulse the walnuts in a food processor to create a fine meal (if there are some bigger pieces, that's okay!).

Melt the chocolate either in a microwave or in a small saucepan on the lowest heat possible, stirring constantly. Set aside to cool.

In the bowl of a stand mixer fitted with the paddle attachment, or in a large bowl, using a whisk, beat together the butter and powdered sugar until soft and creamy. Next, mix in the flour, salt and walnut meal.

Beat in the egg. Then, pour in the melted chocolate and mix to combine. The mixture should thicken slightly.

(CONTINUED)

ASSEMBLE THE TART

Line a 9- to 9½-inch (23- to 24-cm) tart mold with the pâte sucrée dough. Spread the chocolate-walnut cake batter on the bottom in an even layer.

Peel and core 3 of the pears.

You have lots of options for the design: Simply cut the pears in half and place on top; slice crosswise, and fan out the slices on top of the batter; or cut lengthwise and arrange in a pattern. Add some or all of the fourth pear, peeled and cored, if needed to fill in any blank space.

Brush the pears with the melted butter.

Preheat your oven to 350°F (175°C).

While your oven is warming up, freeze the tart for 10 to 15 minutes or chill in the fridge for 20 minutes, to firm up the tart crust, then bake for about 30 minutes. To know when it's done, watch to see whether the chocolate-walnut cake has puffed up and cracked in some places and whether the tart crust is pulling away from the sides of the pan. Check the middle as well, inserting a toothpick to see whether it comes out clean.

MAKE THE WALNUT-CARAMEL SAUCE

Follow the recipe on page 159, stirring in the walnut halves, adding any spices at the end. Set aside to cool and thicken.

Serve the tart either barely warm or at room temperature, drizzled with the walnut-caramel sauce or on its own.

If the caramel sauce is too thick, warm it briefly in a microwave or a small saucepan on low heat.

STORAGE

Keep chilled for up to 3 days.

MAKE AHEAD

Prepare the pâte sucrée in advance. The chocolate-walnut cake batter can be made two days ahead and kept in the fridge.

NOTES

Anjou pears, also known as Beurré d'Anjou, are great for this recipe. This roughly translates to "buttery pears of Anjou," the name of the region in the Loire Valley where they are said to have originated. Bosc pears are a good choice, too.

This recipe calls for 3 to 4 pears, as the size of pears can vary. Start by preparing three and then decide whether you'll need the fourth.

To make this tart gluten-free, omit the tart crust and bake it in an 8-inch (20-cm) greased cake pan. Replace the flour in the recipe with more ground walnuts.

LUNETTES DE ROMANS COOKIES

⚜ MAKES 20 COOKIES ⚜

You've probably heard of the classic Austrian Linzer cookie, but did you know that the French have something similar? Lunettes de Romans were developed in the Middle Ages in the small French town of Romans-sur-Isère. The cookie's name is a combination of the name of the town and what they look like—*lunettes* (eyeglasses)! The cookies are traditionally two stacked oval shapes sandwiched together with jam. The top cookie has two holes cut out like eyeglass lenses for the jam to peek through. They are utterly delicious and something fun to get the whole family involved.

1 recipe Pâte Sucrée (page 17), with the following additions: ½ tsp of ground cinnamon and the zest of 1 orange to the dry ingredients

Baking spray (optional)

All-purpose flour, for dusting

About ¼ cup (80 g) store-bought or homemade jam (traditionally blueberry or strawberry, but it's your choice)

Powdered sugar, to decorate

Make the pâte sucrée dough, adding in the cinnamon and orange zest with the dry ingredients. Chill 45 minutes to 1 hour before proceeding with the recipe.

Preheat your oven to 325°F (165°C). Lightly spray a baking sheet with baking spray or line it with parchment paper or a silicone baking mat.

Roll out the pâte sucrée dough on a floured surface to just under ¼ inch (6 mm) in thickness. Use an oval-shaped cookie cutter—3¼ inches (8 cm) in diameter the long way—to cut out all the dough. Line up the shapes on the prepared baking sheet. I do two lines down the middle so it's easy to make sure that each has a mate.

Use a smaller cookie cutter to cut out and remove two circles from half of the dough ovals. This will allow for the jam to show once the two shapes are sandwiched. I used a small flower-shaped cookie cutter that was about 1 inch (2.5 cm) across. The traditional way is to cut out two small circles, like eyeglass lenses, but you can do whatever you want! The size of the hole doesn't matter. Use the dough scraps to make more cookies.

Bake for 15 to 20 minutes, or until lightly browned around the edges.

Remove from the oven and let cool completely on the baking sheet. Spread a thin layer (about a teaspoon) of jam on the solid cookie halves. Dust the cookie halves with the shapes cut out with powdered sugar and then sandwich on top of the cookies spread with jam.

STORAGE

For the crispiest cookies, eat on the day they are assembled. Store in the fridge in an airtight container for several days; keep in mind that they will soften from the jam.

MAKE AHEAD

Prepare the pâte sucrée dough with the additional add-ins several days ahead. The cookies can be baked 1 week in advance and stored in an airtight container at room temperature before being sandwiched together with jam.

NOTE

Feel free to make these with whatever cookie cutters you like. All you need is two cookies of the same shape so they can be stacked. In my classes for children, they often make dinosaur- or star-shaped cutouts for their lunettes!

BLACKBERRY TART WITH HONEY AND HAZELNUTS

❧ SERVES 6 TO 8 ❧

I filled my market basket with a couple *barquettes* (berry cartons) of blackberries one Saturday and hurried back to my kitchen. The final concoction ended up being this gorgeous tart that is quite the showstopper. As in many French pastries, there are several layers of flavor, adding interest and making it something quite special to enjoy. The fresh blackberries are paired with a creamy honey pastry cream and a layer of soft buttery hazelnut cake baked inside a tart shell. Each layer is easy in itself and can be made in advance, making the assembly in the end a cinch. For a special touch, decorate the finished tarts with fresh elderflowers, when in season, or a drizzle of honey.

½ recipe Pâte Sucrée (page 17)

HONEY PASTRY CREAM

PASTRY CREAM THICKENER

2 large egg yolks

¼ cup (60 ml) honey (see Notes)

1 tbsp (8 g) all-purpose flour

1 tbsp (8 g) cornstarch

2 tbsp (30 ml) whole milk

PASTRY CREAM LIQUIDS

⅔ cup (160 ml) whole milk

½ tbsp (7 g) unsalted butter, at room temperature

1 tsp granulated sugar

HAZELNUT CAKE

2 tbsp (28 g) unsalted butter, at room temperature

¼ cup (30 g) powdered sugar

⅓ cup (30 g) hazelnut flour or meal (finely ground hazelnuts; see Notes)

2 tsp (4 g) all-purpose flour

1 large egg yolk

3½ cups (450 g) fresh blackberries

Start by preparing the pâte sucrée dough so it has time to chill for at least 45 minutes while preparing the rest of the components.

MAKE THE HONEY PASTRY CREAM

For detailed pastry cream tips, see page 35.

Prepare the pastry cream thickener: In a medium-sized bowl, mix together the egg yolks, then whisk in the honey, followed by the flour and cornstarch, and finally, the 2 tablespoons (30 ml) of milk. Set aside.

Prepare the pastry cream liquids: In a medium-sized saucepan, combine the ⅔ cup (160 ml) of milk, butter and sugar. Heat over medium heat, stirring occasionally. When it starts to simmer, take off the heat and slowly pour into the thickening mixture while whisking.

Return everything to the saucepan in one fell swoop and whisk quickly until it thickens and boils. Once it comes to a boil, make sure to whisk for an additional 30 seconds. This is very important as it will ensure that it sets.

Pour into a clean bowl and cover with plastic wrap, in contact with the surface of the pastry cream to prevent a skin from forming on top. Let cool completely in the fridge, about 1 hour.

MAKE THE HAZELNUT CAKE

I recommend making the hazelnut cake batter by hand if your butter is super soft (I leave my butter out for at least an hour before starting this recipe). If mixing with a stand mixer, use the paddle attachment and scrape down the sides several times throughout the process.

In a bowl, whisk (or beat) the butter and powdered sugar until soft and creamy. Then, mix in the ground hazelnuts and flour, followed by the egg yolk. Place in the fridge while you prepare the tart crust.

ASSEMBLE THE TART

Preheat your oven to 325°F (165°C).

Roll out the pâte sucrée dough and line either a 9- to 9½-inch (23 to 24-cm) tart mold or six 4-inch (10-cm) individual molds.

Spoon the chilled hazelnut cake batter inside the tart crust(s) and smooth evenly across the base in a thin layer. Chill for 15 minutes in the fridge or for 10 minutes in the freezer, then bake for 20 to 25 minutes, or until nicely browned across the entire surface. For individual tarts, reduce the baking time to 15 minutes.

Remove from the oven and let cool completely either at room temperature or in the fridge to speed up the process.

Remove the honey pastry cream from the fridge; it will have a gel-like texture after cooling. Before using, whisk briskly by hand just until smooth.

Spread a layer of honey pastry cream over the cooled tart(s), using the back of a spoon or an offset metal spatula. Top with a mound of fresh blackberries and serve.

STORAGE

Keep chilled in the fridge for up to 2 days.

MAKE AHEAD

Prepare the honey pastry cream 3 to 5 days in advance. Keep chilled. Make the pâte sucrée tart dough 3 days ahead. A frozen and thawed tart crust can be used as well. The hazelnut cake batter can be made 2 days in advance.

*See photo on page 14.

NOTES

Use a local honey with a pronounced flavor. You want it to sing in the pastry cream!

Almond flour can be substituted for the hazelnut flour. Hazelnut flour can be found online or at health food or grocery stores by brands such as Bob's Red Mill. To make hazelnut flour, measure ⅓ cup (30 g) of whole hazelnuts and pulse in a food processor until they are finely ground.

CRÈME PÂTISSIÈRE: A SCRUMPTIOUS CUSTARD FILLING

Crème pâtissière is one of the building blocks of many of my favorite French pastries. It is piped between flaky puff pastry for Classic Mille-Feuilles (page 144), baked into a crust to make a Vanilla Bean Flan (page 37) or spread into a tart crust and topped with fresh berries for a Classic Mixed Berry Tart (page 44). It's adaptable and delectable. I've been known to sneak a spoonful straight from the bowl!

It's easy to change the flavor of pastry cream to make your own creations. For example, imagine, in mille-feuilles, instead of using all vanilla pastry cream, dividing the pastry cream and flavoring half of it to be chocolate! *Oui!*

But what is pastry cream? It's a type of custard thickened with egg yolks for richness and a little flour and cornstarch for stability.

BASE RECIPE: VANILLA PASTRY CREAM

❦ MAKES 1¹/₂ CUPS (360 ML) ❧

When I first learned how to make pastry cream at Le Cordon Bleu Paris, it took me several tries to really master it. It was a technique I'd never learned before, and it also involved making it by feel, adding a bit of the sugar here, a bit of the milk there. I've made it much easier by including the exact proportions. The first section of the ingredients (egg yolks, etc.) lists those that thicken the liquids (the second section) into a custard. Follow this recipe step by step and you've got it. It's always surprising how fast it comes together, too! Twenty minutes, max, is all the time you need to make this luscious base.

Psst. Any leftover pastry cream is fabulous enjoyed simply with fresh berries.

PASTRY CREAM THICKENERS
3 egg yolks
¼ cup (50 g) granulated sugar
2 tbsp (15 g) all-purpose flour
1 tbsp (10 g) cornstarch
¼ cup (60 ml) whole milk

PASTRY CREAM LIQUIDS
1 cup (240 ml) whole milk
1 tbsp (14 g) unsalted butter, room temperature, cubed
2 tsp (10 g) granulated sugar
Vanilla: Either ½ tbsp vanilla paste, 1 tbsp vanilla extract or ½–1 vanilla bean (scrape the seeds out and add seeds and pod to the pot)

In a medium-sized bowl, start by vigorously whisking together the egg yolks and ¼ cup (50 g) of granulated sugar for 30 seconds, or until the mixture slightly lightens in color. This is referred to as blanching. Next, whisk in the flour and cornstarch, then, carefully, ¼ cup (60 ml) of milk. This will loosen up the mixture, making it easier to incorporate with the pastry cream liquids later. Adding the ingredients in this order will prevent lumps.

In a medium-sized saucepan, combine the 1 cup (240 ml) of milk, butter, 2 teaspoons (10 g) of sugar, and your choice of vanilla flavoring. The small amount of sugar will keep the milk from scalding. Heat over medium heat. Whisk once or twice to help the sugar dissolve, but otherwise, simply wait until the mixture slowly heats, coming to a simmer. The gradual rise in temperature allows for better flavor infusion of the vanilla. Don't let it bubble away for long or some of the delicious flavor can be lost.

When the milk just comes to a simmer, turn off the heat. Slowly pour into the egg yolk mixture while whisking.

TIP
It helps to put a damp tea towel under the bowl with the pastry cream thickeners or use a bowl with a silicone bottom, to keep it from moving. By slowly pouring in the hot milk, you are tempering the eggs (bringing both mixtures to the same temperature) so the eggs won't cook.

(CONTINUED)

Return everything to the saucepan. (One fell swoop! No slow pouring, or it will spill!) Increase the heat to medium-high and whisk strongly for several minutes. When the mixture thickens and boils, whisk for an additional 30 seconds. Sometimes it's hard to see the boil unless you stop whisking for a couple of seconds to look for the big plops coming to the surface. It is very important to whisk while the mixture boils for 30 seconds, or your pastry cream might not set.

The finished texture will be smooth and thick like pudding. Pour into a clean bowl. Cover with plastic wrap, touching the surface of the pastry cream. This helps it cool faster and prevents a skin from forming on top. Chill until cold, about 1 hour.

When you're ready to use the cooled pastry cream, you'll find the texture is like jelly. Whisk by hand just until it's smooth—this only takes a minute. Whisk too long and you can loosen the firm structure too much and it might start to get runny.

MAKE AHEAD

Pastry cream can be made 3 to 5 days in advance, depending on the expiration date of your milk. If made with super-fresh milk, it will last for 5 days, no problem.

NOTE

There is a huge variation in the amount of vanilla added to pastry cream, from pretty reasonable to quite extraordinary (imagine 3 vanilla beans in this recipe). Using a whole vanilla bean in this recipe really amplifies the vanilla flavor.

OPTIONAL INSURANCE POLICY

After the pastry cream is cooked, look at the texture. If you don't see any little bits or lumps that you want to strain out, then no need. But if you do, straining the pastry cream after you finish cooking it will help make sure it's completely smooth. Strain the pastry cream by placing a strainer on top of a clean bowl and pour the cooked hot pastry cream directly into it. Pick up the strainer and rub a spatula inside across the wire to push the mixture through. Make sure to scrape the underside, too!

PASTRY CREAM VARIATIONS

Pastry cream transforms in consistency when mixed with butter, meringue or cream.

The classic variations are:

- **Diplomate:** pastry cream + whipped cream
- **Frangipane:** pastry cream + almond cream
- **Mousseline:** pastry cream + butter
- **Chiboust:** pastry cream and gelatin + Italian meringue

The flavor adaptations are endless, but here are some ideas. To the base vanilla pastry cream recipe, remove the vanilla (or reduce it), and substitute:

- **Chocolate:** Add a big handful (¼ cup [50 g]) of chopped bittersweet, semisweet or milk chocolate to the hot pastry cream right after you finish cooking it. Whisk in the chocolate to melt and combine. Add more to taste.
- **Fruit:** Get creative and add different fruit purees or jams. Let the pastry cream cool completely, then whisk it in. Start with 3 tablespoons (45 ml), then add to taste.
- **Lavender or other herbs:** Add a sprig of fresh lavender or another fresh herb, such as mint, to the milk at the beginning; ¼ teaspoon of culinary-grade dried lavender buds works, too. This will infuse the flavor into the milk as it heats. Strain at the end and taste. If you'd like a stronger taste, add the herbs back in and infuse the mixture for longer as it chills.
- **Coffee:** Add 1 tablespoon (6 g) of instant espresso powder to the thickening ingredients at the beginning.

VANILLA BEAN FLAN

❧ SERVES 8 TO 10 ❧

Flans have been served since the Middle Ages, when they were considered a fashionable addition to a feast. Can't you just see this next to a tower of fruit while a lute is strummed in the background? Nowadays, it's often offered as a simple dessert to accompany your baguette sandwich from the boulangerie.

The pastry cream filling is just slightly different than the base recipe (page 35) as it includes whole eggs and egg yolks, and it undeniably needs a vanilla bean or two. The method remains practically the same with a change here and there due to the quantity and because it will be baked.

It's almost like a science experiment, watching it bake. The top layer of the pastry cream filling separates and balloons up, creating the iconic charred appearance that makes everyone ooh and aah. Don't worry—it doesn't taste burnt, though! The inside is an incredibly luscious cooked custard speckled with vanilla bean seeds.

PÂTE BRISÉE SUCRÉE
1½ cups + 1 tbsp (200 g) all-purpose flour
2 tsp (10 g) granulated sugar
½ tsp salt
7 tbsp (100 g) unsalted butter, cold, cubed
1 large egg
1 tsp water
½ tsp vanilla extract

VANILLA BEAN PASTRY CREAM FILLING
PASTRY CREAM LIQUIDS
1¾ cups (420 ml) heavy cream
3 cups (720 ml) whole milk
1 to 2 vanilla beans (your choice!)

PASTRY CREAM THICKENER
3 large eggs, at room temperature
3 large egg yolks
1¼ cups (250 g) granulated sugar
¾ cup (95 g) cornstarch

MAKE THE PÂTE BRISÉE SUCRÉE

The method is the same as the pâte sucrée dough, but the dough is less sweet, to balance with the custard filling. Refer to the pâte sucrée recipe for additional tips and photos of specific steps (page 17).

In a bowl, combine the flour, sugar and salt. Mix together with a clean hand. Add the cold butter and toss with the flour mixture to coat.

Incorporate the butter either using a pastry blender or working it in by hand until the butter is in small pieces. The motion you'll make is what one of my chef instructors called "show me the money": Scoop up the flour mixture with both palms facing up, and then press the butter pieces with your thumb moving along slightly open fingertips. This smears and presses the butter, breaking it into smaller pieces and mixing it with the dry ingredients.

Repeat this motion until all the butter is about pea-sized. If there are several large pieces, that's not a big deal. Add the egg, water and vanilla extract, and use a finger or fork to mix them in (this way, the rest of your hand doesn't get super dirty).

(CONTINUED)

VANILLA BEAN FLAN (CONTINUED)

Empty out into a mound on a clean surface. Using the bottom part of your palm (closest to your wrist) and, starting at the top of the pile, farthest from you, press and smear the dough forward and away from you in multiple strokes, streaking the mixture across the work surface.

Once you've worked your way through all the dough, scrape together into a pile (a plastic dough scraper is great for this) and start again, repeating until the dough comes together. The amount of times you will have to do this depends on the temperature of your ingredients and kitchen.

Wrap in plastic wrap and chill for at least 45 minutes before rolling out and shaping to the springform pan.

PREPARE THE PAN

Roll out the dough into a large, very thin circle. Hold a 9-inch (23-cm) springform pan over the dough to make sure it's big enough to go all the way up the sides once it's molded inside. Fold the dough in half and ease it into the mold (no need to butter it). Press the dough into the corners and to the top of the mold. Doing a bit of patchwork to make this happen is A-okay! Some of the dough around the sides might not lie perfectly flat. Just press any pleats flush against the side. Use a knife to cut off the excess dough from around the top cutting from the inside, outward. Place in the freezer.

Preheat your oven to 400°F (200°C) so it is ready to go because once the pastry cream is done, the flan will need to go straight into the oven.

MAKE THE VANILLA BEAN PASTRY CREAM

Prepare the pastry cream liquids: Pour the cream and milk into a big saucepan. Cut open the vanilla bean(s) and scrape out the seeds, adding them to the liquid. Throw in the pod(s) for extra flavor.

Place the saucepan over low heat to start warming up the milk mixture and infusing it with the vanilla.

Meanwhile, prepare the pastry cream thickener: In a big bowl, combine the eggs and yolks and whisk well together, then add the sugar. Whisk to combine, then stir in the cornstarch.

Increase the heat of the milk mixture, bringing it just to a simmer. Don't let it simmer for long, as then the liquid will start to evaporate.

Turn off the heat and pour about half of the hot milk mixture into the egg mixture. Whisk well. This will temper the eggs, bringing them to the same temperature as the milk mixture. In a single confident motion, pour the egg mixture into the saucepan containing the remaining milk mixture, so everything is now in the same pot. Whisk well and then turn the heat back on to medium. Take out those arm muscles and WHISK! Whisk for several minutes, until the mixture thickens and boils. You'll need to whisk strongly! You might break a sweat! Maybe have a friend nearby to help.

(CONTINUED)

As soon as the pastry cream boils (large bubbles will plop to the surface), remove from the heat.

Quickly take the pastry-lined springform pan out of the freezer. Remove the vanilla bean pod(s) from the pastry cream and pour the cream into the mold, smoothing the top. If it looks as if the top of the pastry cream has cooled and formed a skin, give it a good whisk before pouring it into the springform pan.

The pastry cream will come to about an inch (2.5 cm) from the top of the pan. It will rise as it bakes and the crust will shrink just a touch for a perfect finish.

BAKE THE FLAN

Bake at 400°F (200°C) for 10 minutes, then lower the heat to 350°F (175°C) and bake for 50 minutes. The top of the flan will rise up like a balloon and become very brown, almost black. Check the crust when the timer goes off and make sure it is nice and brown, and bake longer, if necessary.

Carefully remove from the oven and let cool at room temperature for several hours, then transfer to the refrigerator for several hours to chill completely (just as you would a cheesecake). The top will deflate and the inside will be nice and creamy.

To enjoy, remove the sides from the springform pan. Eat chilled or at room temperature.

STORAGE

Keep in the fridge. The flan will easily last for 5 days, unless it disappears before then!

MAKE AHEAD

This is best made the day before so it has plenty of time to chill.

Prepare the pâte brisée sucrée in advance. You can even form the crust to the springform pan and freeze it until you are ready to fill. Keep the dough up to 2 days in the refrigerator, or a month in the freezer.

NOTE

It's important to use a good sturdy whisk. Not one whose handle is going to come off when making the pastry cream. Not that this has ever happened to me, huh hum. This recipe yields a large quantity of pastry cream and will certainly give your arm a workout.

STRAWBERRY FRAISIER

❧ SERVES 10 TO 12 ❧

A staple at French pâtisseries during summer! For this iconic cake, strawberries proudly stand around the edge between two rounds of light génoise cake. The visual is spectacular, making it ideal for a special occasion. The inside is a beautiful mixture of rich vanilla bean mousseline (pastry cream whipped with butter) and sliced fresh strawberries.

Fraisier can be a little intimidating to make, so let's break it down: It's a layered cake with a bit of pizzazz going into the decoration and assembly which, I think, makes it quite fun!

VANILLA MOUSSELINE CREAM
1 recipe Vanilla Pastry Cream (page 35) (see Note)
14 tbsp (1½ sticks + 2 tbsp [200 g]) unsalted, soft room-temperature butter, cubed

GÉNOISE
Baking spray, for pan
1 recipe Layered Génoise Cake (page 105)

SIMPLE SYRUP
½ cup (100 g) granulated sugar
½ cup (120 ml) water
Optional: 1 to 2 tbsp (15 to 30 ml) kirsch or other liqueur, or 2 tbsp (30 ml) strawberry puree

TO DECORATE
1 lb (3 cups [450 g]) fresh whole strawberries, divided
Chopped pistachios (optional)

CHANTILLY CREAM
1½ cups (360 ml) heavy cream, cold
¼ cup (30 g) powdered sugar
1 tsp vanilla extract, or ½ tsp vanilla paste

Make the Vanilla Pastry Cream (page 35) and chill completely in the fridge, about 1 hour.

MAKE THE GÉNOISE
Preheat your oven to 325°F (165°C) and spray a 9-inch (23-cm) springform pan with baking spray. Cut a circle of parchment paper to fit in the bottom and spray the top of this, too.

Prepare the layered génoise cake batter and pour into the prepared springform pan. Then, bake for 30 to 35 minutes until golden brown on top and pulling away slightly from the sides. Remove from the oven and let cool completely at room temperature.

PREPARE THE SIMPLE SYRUP
In a small saucepan, simply boil the granulated sugar, water and the liqueur or fruit puree (if using) until the sugar has dissolved. This will add moisture to the cake. Set aside to cool.

MAKE THE VANILLA MOUSSELINE CREAM
Take the prepared pastry cream out of the fridge. Give it a good whisk by hand for a nice smooth texture.

(CONTINUED)

In the bowl of a stand mixer fitted with the whisk attachment, or using a large bowl and an electric hand mixer, whip the soft butter for several minutes, until smooth and very soft, like mayonnaise. Slowly add the pastry cream to the butter, a small spoonful at a time, while whipping on high speed. Wait for each addition to be fully incorporated before adding the next. As it's hard to see, I simply count to ten after each addition before plopping in the next. Scrape down the bowl a couple of times throughout. At the end, whip several minutes on high speed to make sure it's nice and fluffy. Then, transfer to a pastry bag fitted with a 10- to 12-mm round tip (or no tip; just cut to a ½-inch [1.3-cm] opening; see chart, page 12).

ASSEMBLE THE CAKE

Run a knife around the inside of the springform pan to release the cake. Open the ring and remove the génoise cake. Wash the ring, close the hinge and place on your serving platter. Line the sides with strips of parchment paper to keep the cake from sticking to the ring. As soon as the cake layer is added, they'll be pushed into position.

Cut the génoise cake in half horizontally, using a serrated knife. Carefully set the top of the cake aside on a piece of parchment, cut side up. Fit the bottom layer of the génoise inside the ring, cut side up. Liberally brush with the simple syrup.

Pick out about 10 strawberries for the outside ring. They should all be about the same height. Hull and slice in half lengthwise. Then, line up with each cut side pressed against the side of the ring and the point of each strawberry facing up. Pipe a swirl of mousseline cream on top of the cake layer, then up the sides and in between the strawberries. It helps to cut the parchment ring at this point to be flush with the top of the pan, so you have more space to pipe. If needed, use an offset spatula or a butter knife to spread the mousseline into the crevices around the strawberries.

Set aside several pretty strawberries to use as decoration. Slice the remaining strawberries and distribute on top of the cream. Swirl the remaining cream on top and smooth with an offset spatula.

Brush the cut side of the top layer of génoise with the simple syrup while it's on the parchment, and then flip it to fit on top. Dab the top of the cake layer with the simple syrup, too.

Chill for 1 hour to set. Wrap the top with plastic wrap to keep the cake fresh for up to 2 days. When ready to decorate, open up and remove the springform band, along with the parchment paper strips.

MAKE THE CHANTILLY WHIPPED CREAM

In the bowl of a stand mixer fitted with the whisk attachment, whip the heavy cream, powdered sugar and vanilla to medium-firm peaks on medium-high speed. Place in a piping bag fitted with a fun piping tip and use to decorate the cake, or simply pile it on top and smooth with a spoon for luscious swirls! Sprinkle with pistachios for color (if using) and top with the reserved strawberries.

Let the cake sit at room temperature for 30 minutes before serving so the mousseline cream has time to soften (it contains a lot of butter, which will be firm when chilled).

MAKE AHEAD

Prepare the pastry cream up to 3 to 5 days in advance. The génoise cake can be made the day before, wrapped well in plastic wrap and stored at room temperature. The cake will keep for 2 days in the fridge once assembled.

NOTE
This is the time to use a vanilla bean in that pastry cream! Trust me, it's worth it!

CLASSIC MIXED BERRY TART

❧ SERVES 6 ❧

The base is a crisp, sweet tart dough filled with creamy pastry cream. Then, the top is loaded up with all different kinds of berries. It's a rich yet light combination perfect for a summer day! There's a little trick to placing the berries to make it oh so appealing: Start with the largest berries and then fill in with the smaller berries. I'll go into more detail in the recipe. Usually for the berries, I purchase a large container of strawberries, then small ones of raspberries, blueberries, and blackberries. You want a nice mix of flavor and color.

This tart is easy to assemble, especially when the tart crust and pastry cream are made in advance.

2 recipes Vanilla Pastry Cream (page 35)
½ recipe Pâte Sucrée (page 17)
4 cups (500 g) mixed berries

Prepare the vanilla pastry cream and pâte sucrée dough. When ready to assemble, blind bake the tart dough as directed in the recipe, using a 9½-inch (24-cm) round tart pan, or a 4 x 14-inch (10 x 35.5–cm) rectangular tart pan.

Remove from the oven and let the crust cool completely. Push up the removable base to detach the crust from the mold. Place on a serving platter. Give the cooled vanilla pastry cream a good whisk by hand for a nice smooth texture. Then, fill the tart crust with the vanilla pastry cream, smoothing it with an offset metal spatula or the back of a spoon.

To decorate, first assess your fruit and pull out several of the showstoppers. These, you'll place on the top as a garnish (this usually includes the cute little strawberries with their tops still on). Set them aside and then randomly place the largest of the remaining fruit (usually strawberries) on top of the pastry cream. This will act as your base. I usually add just about all of the strawberries, some cut in half and quarters and others left whole (it's nice to have a mix) in various angles to add dimension. Then, fill in with the other berries, finishing with the reserved showstoppers.

STORAGE
Keep chilled. Lasts 2 days.

MAKE AHEAD
Follow the pastry cream and pâte sucrée make ahead instructions. The tart dough can be precooked and kept at room temperature for up to a week in an airtight container before assembling.

NOTE
For a shimmer of gold: Add a touch of gold luster dust or gold leaf, as seen in this photo.

VARIATION
Lavender Pastry Cream: Add ½ teaspoon of culinary-grade dried lavender buds with the milk at the beginning of the pastry cream recipe, and reduce the vanilla by half. Strain the buds out of the mixture or keep them in! You want the lavender flavor to stand up to the fresh fruit but not overpower it.

GANACHE AU CHOCOLAT:
A SAUCE, A FILLING AND A STAND-ALONE TREAT!

Ganache is one of my favorite recipes for you to have in your apron pocket! You can use it in so many baking situations: to glaze cakes, fill tarts, macarons and cookies, pour over ice cream, spread as frosting and roll to make truffles! It's even used as a base for desserts, such as The Frenchman's Chocolate Mousse (page 123) and Moelleux au Chocolat (page 59).

A ganache is an emulsion (like salad dressing!) that brings together two things that don't really want to be together (liquid and chocolate). The classic method is to heat cream just to a simmer and then pour it over the chocolate. Wait a couple of minutes for the chocolate to start melting and then stir to combine.

Depending on the temperature, your ganache will be at different consistencies. For example, a hot ganache is liquid enough to pour, but not firm enough to pipe between cookies. It is traditionally made with cream, but it can be made with all sorts of liquids, including fruit purees and even caramel (see Chocolate-Caramel-Nut Tart, page 166). This changes the flavor and the textures, making ganache even more interesting!

BASE RECIPE: CHOCOLATE SAUCE FOR ALL OCCASIONS

MAKES 1¹/₂ CUPS (360 ML)

First and foremost, this is the perfect chocolate sauce to pour over ice cream while it's still a bit warm. It cools on contact, making the most delectably fudgy chocolate addition to any scoop!

You can also drizzle it over a cake right after it's made for a drizzle drip finish—divine! Or use it as an icing, letting it cool to spreadable consistency. I'd also recommend making a batch for *chocolat chaud* (hot chocolate!): Add big scoops of the cooled sauce to mugs and top with hot milk. Stir to combine and top with marshmallows for the ultimate chocolate fix! And did I say it's as easy as combining two ingredients?

6 oz (170 g) bittersweet, dark or semisweet chocolate (60 to 70%), chopped
1 cup (240 ml) heavy cream

Place the chocolate in a medium-sized bowl. It always helps to chop the chocolate, no matter if it's already in chips. The smaller pieces make it easier to melt and combine.

Heat the cream until it starts simmering and then pour it, all in one go, over the chocolate. Wiggle the bowl to fully cover the chocolate pieces with the cream. Let sit for a couple minutes for the chocolate to start to melt. Stirring immediately will cool everything down before it's had a chance to melt. Then, whisk in the center—first gently, so the liquid doesn't fly out of the bowl, then briskly once it thickens, to bring it all together and form an emulsion. At first it will look separated, then it will come together into a thick, glossy chocolate sauce.

If you have a couple of chocolate pieces that haven't melted, gently warm in a microwave or place the bowl (be sure it is heatproof) on top of a saucepan of steaming water to make a double boiler.

HOW TO USE IT

Use immediately to pour over ice cream, or for a slightly thicker sauce, let cool at room temperature for several minutes. To use as a filling in between cookies or cakes, let cool at room temperature until it is thick enough to spread. Reheat as needed with short blasts in a microwave, or in a small saucepan on the lowest heat, stirring constantly (it won't take much!).

STORAGE

Ganache can be kept in the fridge in an airtight container or covered with plastic wrap, touching the surface, for 1 week or frozen for 1 month.

(CONTINUED)

NOTE

The type of chocolate in your ganache determines how much cream is added. This means you can't flip-flop types of chocolate in ganache recipes, or the result will be different. For example, if you add the same quantity of cream to bittersweet and milk chocolate, the ganache made with the milk chocolate will be runnier because of the higher overall amount of dairy in the ganache coming from that which is in the milk chocolate bar.

CHOCOLATE BRAND RECOMMENDATIONS

Use good-quality chocolate for all ganaches! Since chocolate is the main flavor, it's important to use a higher-end chocolate. Look for Valrhona, Guittard, Ghiradelli, Cacao Barry, Lindt, Scharffen Berger or Callebaut.

Use bar chocolate when possible, or higher-quality chips.

GANACHE FIXES

Split/grainy/oily: The emulsion hasn't occurred. Try whisking energetically first—often, this will fix it. If this doesn't work, try stirring in a tablespoon (15 ml) of warm milk, a little at a time, until smooth. You can also melt the whole mixture completely in a double boiler, stirring constantly.

Lumpy: This often means that the chocolate hasn't melted completely. Heat in a microwave, or heat briefly in a double boiler, stirring constantly.

Too thin: Stir in melted chocolate to the correct consistency.

Too thick: Stir in hot cream to the correct consistency.

Too hard/cold: If it's in a piping bag, massage the mixture to warm it up. If it's in a bowl, let sit at room temperature until it's the right consistency. You can also try briefly microwaving it at 10- to 15-second bursts, then stirring to distribute the heat. Remember—it doesn't take much! Also, it could mean that the next time you make it, you might need to add a little more cream to the mixture because of the brand/type of chocolate you used.

VARIATIONS

Add a big pinch of salt!

Boozy: Replace 1 to 2 tablespoons (15 to 30 ml) of the cream with booze (Baileys, Armangnac, rum . . .). Stir in at the end.

Coffee: Add 1 tablespoon (6 g) of instant espresso powder to the cream while heating.

Fruit: Replace the cream with a fruit puree. Melt the chocolate, then stir in the puree.

Peanut butter: Replace one-quarter of the cream with creamy peanut butter. Whisk in at the end.

Peppermint: Add ½ teaspoon of peppermint extract or more to taste, or infuse the cream with fresh mint.

TIGRÉ ALMOND CAKES

 MAKES 12 CAKES

A classic pastry that you rarely find in pastry shops now, the tigré is named for its tigerlike appearance. The base is a financier, a butter almond cake, speckled with chocolate pieces; the inside, a fabulous soft chocolate ganache. It might look more like a leopard than a tiger, but that sure doesn't bother me! I've come up with a way to replicate it at home with no special molds required. These are fun and easy, and I think you'll be happily surprised with the results.

ALMOND CAKE BATTER

8 tbsp (1 stick [115 g]) unsalted butter, cubed

⅔ cup (60 g) almond flour or meal

1 cup + 2 tbsp (140 g) powdered sugar

⅓ cup (45 g) all-purpose flour

4 large egg whites (~120 g)

½ tsp vanilla extract

1.5 oz (45 g) bittersweet or semisweet chocolate, finely chopped (see Notes)

Baking spray or melted unsalted butter, for pan

CHOCOLATE GANACHE

2 oz (60 g) bittersweet or semisweet chocolate, chopped

¼ cup (60 ml) heavy cream

PREPARE THE ALMOND CAKE BATTER

Brown the butter: Place the cubed butter in a small to medium-sized saucepan with a light-colored interior (so you can see the color change) over low to medium heat. Swirl the pan until all the butter is melted. This also helps a bit with some of the sputtering (be careful!).

Once the butter is melted, continue to heat it on the stove. At first, there will be big bubbles, then this changes to smaller bubbles, and eventually it foams. Watch for the first signs of browning on the bottom of the pan. You may need to angle the pan to see this.

As soon as you see browning, remove the pan from the stove. The butter will continue to cook with the residual heat for the next several minutes. By turning off the heat at the first sign of browning, you'll prevent it from burning. Set aside to cool.

Into a large bowl, pour the almond flour, powdered sugar and flour. Whisk together and then whisk in the egg whites and vanilla. Mix well to get out any lumps.

Next, pour in the browned butter and carefully whisk into the batter. Then, stir the chopped chocolate into the batter (even the chocolate dust). Cover and let chill for at least 1 hour or up to 3 days, to firm up.

When you're ready to bake the tigré, preheat your oven to 350°F (175°C).

(CONTINUED)

Spray a standard 12-well muffin tin (or mini doughnut pan; see Notes) with baking spray or brush with melted butter. Divide the batter equally among the wells, filling them one-quarter of the way full. Place a piece of parchment paper on top of the muffin tin, then top with a flat sturdy baking sheet. This will encase the cakes during the baking process so you will have flat cakes, instead of domed.

Bake for 20 minutes, then remove the baking sheet and parchment paper. Bake for another 3 to 5 minutes, or until the sides are browned and pulling away from the sides. Remove from the oven, let cool for 5 minutes in the tin and then turn out onto a clean surface.

Use the back of a teaspoon-sized measuring spoon to firmly press into the bottom of each warm cake to make an indentation. Sometimes you need to try a second time for the indentation to stay. Be sure to do this while the cakes are still warm.

WHILE THE CAKES COOL, MAKE THE CHOCOLATE GANACHE FILLING

Place the chocolate in a small bowl. Heat the cream just to slmmering on the stove or in a microwave and pour, all in one go, over the chocolate. Wiggle the bowl to make sure all the chocolate is covered, then let it sit for a couple of minutes for the chocolate to start to melt.

Stir the chocolate and heavy cream together with a whisk, gently at first, then briskly to bring it together.

Transfer to a piping bag and cut a small opening at the end. Pipe into the indentation you made in the cakes, or simply spoon it in. Let cool several minutes before using if it's too runny to control.

Let the chocolate set at room temperature (about 30 minutes to an hour) or enjoy immediately for a runny center.

STORAGE
Keep in an airtight container at room temperature for up to 3 days.

MAKE AHEAD
Whip up the cake batter up to 2 days in advance.

NOTES
For the chocolate, you can use mini chocolate chips, or baking chocolate in bar, disk or chip form. In all cases, though, I would recommend chopping the chocolate into very small pieces to achieve the look of these cakes.

Usually tigré are made in a special mold that makes an indentation in the middle of the cake to fill with the chocolate ganache. In this recipe, we use a standard muffin tin and a special method to replicate this. You can also make them in a mini doughnut pan. If baking in a mini doughnut pan, make sure to use enough batter to go over the middle indentation. These will take about 15 minutes to bake.

ONE-BITE CHOCOLATE TRUFFLES

 MAKES 20

Truffles are the ultimate chocolate ganache indulgence. Use this as a base recipe to make different flavors and a guide for different delicious things to roll them in. The world is your oyster, or should I say chocolate box! I love to make them for friends for the holidays or as an after-dinner treat with an espresso. These are super easy and a fun activity for everyone to get involved in.

8 oz (225 g) bittersweet or semisweet chocolate (60 to 70%), roughly chopped

3 tbsp (40 g) unsalted butter, cubed, at room temperature

¾ cup (180 ml) heavy cream

TOPPING OPTIONS

Unsweetened cocoa powder, sprinkles, toasted unsweetened coconut flakes, finely chopped and toasted nuts, chocolate shavings, freeze-dried fruit powder such as raspberry, melted chocolate or ganache

Melt the chocolate and butter together either in the microwave or by placing them in a bowl over a steaming pot of water to create a double boiler.

Heat the cream in a saucepan or in the microwave until it just starts to simmer. Pour the cream into the chocolate and whisk to combine.

Cover the ganache with plastic wrap so the wrap is touching the surface, to prevent condensation dripping into the chocolate, and chill for 1 to 2 hours (or even up to overnight), until firm but pliable. Check the texture by scooping some of the chocolate. If it is easy to scoop and holding its shape, it's at a good temperature. How long it needs to chill entirely depends on your fridge and how shallow and/or wide the container you're using is. If it is too hard and is breaking into big pieces as you scoop it, let it warm up at room temperature, about 15 minutes.

FORM THE TRUFFLES

Making truffles is a sticky business! To avoid the warmth of your hands, use a small scoop the size of your choice (I use a 1-tablespoon [15-ml] or #60 scoop). Drop the scoops directly into the topping you've chosen. I don't mind the slightly rough edge from the scoop and it's usually hidden by the topping.

For a nice round truffle: Scoop the ganache either with a scoop or spoon and roll between your fingertips (it will be messy!), then toss in the topping of your choice.

After decorating, chill to set, about 30 minutes.

STORAGE

The truffles will last for about 3 days in an airtight container in the fridge. Take out at least 15 minutes before eating for the chill to dissipate and the texture to be nice and soft. Freeze for up to a month.

NOTES

Use the best chocolate you can find, as this is the main ingredient. See suggestions for brands on page 50. See the ganache variations on page 50 for how to further change the flavor (such as by adding Baileys or peppermint extract).

This recipe can easily be doubled or tripled.

EARL GREY MADELEINES

 MAKES 24

The beauty of these buttery cakes is that they can be made by hand quite easily. They have a distinctive shape, which, when made well, has a signature bump on top that is called a *bosse*. The bosse forms from the oven heat concentrating on the curve of the shell-shaped madeleine mold. People think this is hard to achieve, but follow a few tips and you'll be the boss of the madeleines.

Earl Grey tea is brought in to flavor the batter of the cakes as well as added to a delicious ganache that is piped inside. This recipe shows a unique way to infuse flavor into a ganache, changing it up from the classic recipe!

MADELEINE CAKES

2 tea bags (2 tsp [4 g]) finely ground Earl Grey tea

14 tbsp (1½ sticks + 2 tbsp [200 g]) unsalted butter, cubed

3 large eggs, at room temperature

¾ cup (150 g) granulated sugar

¼ cup (60 ml) whole milk

1½ cups (200 g) all-purpose flour, plus more for dusting

Pinch of salt

1½ tsp (7 g) baking powder

Soft unsalted butter, for tin

EARL GREY MILK CHOCOLATE GANACHE

⅓ cup (80 ml) heavy cream

1 tea bag (1 tsp) Earl Grey tea

4 oz (115 g) milk chocolate, chopped

MAKE THE MADELEINE CAKES

Cut open the tea bags (make sure the tea is finely ground) and pour the tea leaves into a small to medium-sized saucepan. Add the butter and melt over medium-low heat, swirling occasionally. Once melted, remove from the heat and set aside as you prepare the rest of the recipe. This will infuse the butter with the tea flavor, just as it would for a cup of tea!

In a big bowl, whisk together the eggs and sugar well by hand for about 30 seconds. Whisk in the milk.

In a separate bowl, by hand, combine the flour, salt and baking powder. Add to the egg mixture in two additions and whisk to combine.

Pour in the melted butter in two additions, whisking until smooth. I like to leave the Earl Grey tea in the batter for a speckled finished cake and more flavor.

(CONTINUED)

You can bake the madeleines now, or cover with plastic wrap and chill for several hours or (even better!) overnight. You'll notice that the batter will firm up after chilling. This makes it easier to put in the molds and helps form the bump!

When you're ready to bake, coat a 12-shell madeleine tin generously with soft butter (I use a crumpled-up paper towel or a brush) and sprinkle each cavity with flour. These cakes tend to stick, so butter even a nonstick tin. A silicone pan doesn't need to be buttered or floured. Hold one end of the pan and tap the center to move the flour around in each mold to coat it. Tap off any excess flour.

Preheat your oven to 375°F (190°C) (convection or standard, with a preference for convection—no need to adjust the temperature) and transfer the batter into a piping bag without a tip. Cut a large opening. Alternatively, you can spoon the batter into the molds or even use a tablespoon-sized (15-ml) scoop.

Transfer the batter into just the middle of each mold, filling it three-quarters of the way full (see picture on page 56).

Place in the freezer for 5 minutes and then put directly into the hot oven. The tin should go straight onto the oven rack, not on a baking sheet, for the best temperature shock to form the bump on top. However, if using a silicone mold, you will need to put it on a baking sheet. For best results, only bake one pan at a time.

Bake for 5 minutes, then lower the heat to 325°F (165°C) and bake for an additional 5 minutes. If using a silicone mold or a nonconvection oven, they might need to bake for 2 to 3 more minutes. Touch the center of a madeleine. The cakes should spring back and they should be nicely browned as well.

As soon as they come out of the oven, unmold the madeleines by inverting the pan onto a clean kitchen towel, tapping the end if necessary.

MAKE THE GANACHE

In a small saucepan, combine the cream and tea (removed from the bag) over medium heat until it just starts to simmer, swirling occasionally. Turn off the heat, cover and allow to infuse for 20 to 30 minutes.

Place the chopped chocolate in a medium bowl.

Return the cream to the heat, bringing the mixture once more to a simmer. Pour through a small sieve (to remove the tea) onto the chopped chocolate.

Whisk together to incorporate, then allow to cool for 10 minutes or so to firm up slightly, which will make the ganache more manageable. Transfer to a piping bag. Use a 5- to 6-mm small round tip (see chart, page 12). Using a tip allows you to puncture the madeleine and fill it with the ganache.

Insert the tip about ¼ inch (6 mm) into the top of a cooled madeleine and fill with ganache. Cut the first one you do in half, to see how well it's filled. This will give you an indication of how much ganache you need to put in each of the others. I usually fill until, when I remove the tip, a little ganache pools out the top, making a cute dot.

Fill the madeleine while the ganache is still warm and fluid. Allow it to firm up for about 30 minutes at room temperature before serving.

STORAGE

Store at room temperature in an airtight container. Normally, madeleines are good for only a day, but with the ganache filling, they stay moist for two!

MAKE AHEAD

Prepare the madeleine batter the day before, for best results. It will last in the fridge for about 2 days.

MOELLEUX AU CHOCOLAT

⚜ MAKES 9 INDIVIDUAL CAKES ⚜

The base of this deliciously fabulous chocolate cake is a chocolate ganache that creates a soft, liquid, lavalike center. How much lava ooze you have is based on personal preference and how long you bake the cake. Each time you make them, note your baking time and whether you liked how runny the center was. For me, they are perfect at 8½ minutes, using the convection setting on my oven. I love a combination of milk and bittersweet chocolate in the batter, too. A bonus is that it's made all by hand in one big bowl!

These are best served warm and are delicious with a scoop of ice cream, fresh berries or a caramel sauce, such as Molly's Favorite Salted Caramel Sauce (page 159).

Baking spray or unsalted butter, for pan or ramekins

7 tbsp (100 g) salted or unsalted butter

7 oz (200 g) bittersweet chocolate (60 to 70%), milk chocolate or a combination of the two

3 large eggs, at room temperature

½ tsp vanilla extract

½ cup (100 g) granulated sugar

¼ cup (30 g) all-purpose flour

Pinch of salt (omit if using salted butter)

Preheat your oven to 400°F (200°C).

Spray either nine wells of a muffin tin or nine individual ramekins with baking spray, or butter them.

Melt the butter and chocolate together, being careful not to burn the chocolate. You can do this in a microwave until melted. Alternatively, using a double boiler is a great method, too: Place the chocolate and butter in a heatproof bowl and set over a saucepan of simmering water. Stir until melted. Let cool for 2 to 3 minutes.

If you microwaved it, transfer the chocolate mixture to a large bowl and whisk in the eggs (if you used the double-boiler method, you'll just have to dry off the bottom of the bowl). The batter will seem runny at first, but as the mixture cools and the eggs incorporate, it will thicken and resemble a brownie or cake batter. You will need to whisk strongly for about 30 seconds to reach this state.

Add the vanilla. Whisk in the sugar, then the flour and salt (if using).

Use a large (¼-cup [60-ml] or #16) scoop or spoon to transfer the batter to the prepared muffin wells or ramekins, filling each well or ramekin three-quarters of the way full. This batter will not rise when baked.

Bake for 8 to 10 minutes, using either the convection or standard setting on your oven. The cakes are done when they are puffed around the edges and the center is a slightly darker color and soft to the touch. Sometimes, they will have small cracks around the edges. The baking time depends on your oven and how gooey a center you want. Keep a close eye on them, starting at 8 minutes.

(CONTINUED)

After removing from the oven, let cool for a couple of minutes.

If you used ramekins, they should be served in the ramekins. To remove from the muffin tin, place a large piece of parchment paper on top of the pan. Place a big cutting board or baking sheet on top of the parchment. Then flip, using two oven mitts! If any cakes stick in the pan, run a knife around the edge to release.

These are best warm from the oven.

STORAGE

Store at room temperature in an airtight container for 2 to 3 days—but they never last that long!

ADDITIONAL FLAVORINGS

Add one of the following, or a combination, with the flour: ½ teaspoon of ground cinnamon, ¼ teaspoon of ground cardamom, 1 tablespoon (6 g) of instant espresso powder, a pinch or two of cayenne pepper or ¼ cup (28 g) of finely chopped toasted pecans or walnuts. You can also pop a fresh raspberry in the center before baking.

NOTE

When making for a party, prepare the batter in advance. Chill the cakes in their muffin tin or ramekins until you are ready to bake them, or store the batter in a bowl if fridge space is at a premium. The perfect time to pop them into the oven is after clearing the table from the main course. Everyone has time to chat for a bit and then there's the anticipation of dessert when an enticing smell starts to waft from the kitchen.

DARK CHOCOLATE GANACHE TART

⚔ SERVES 8 TO 10 ⚔

This tart is rich, utterly delicious and incredibly easy to make. A gorgeously smooth chocolate ganache is poured into a prebaked tart shell, *et voilà*! Set aside to firm up at room temperature (or speed this up in the fridge), decorate and serve. There are lots of different ways to decorate the tart, as the ganache offers the perfect blank canvas. I've included several ideas for toppings in the recipe. No matter how you decide to finish the tart, it will be quite the stunner!

½ recipe chocolate or vanilla Pâte Sucrée (page 17)

10 oz (285 g) bittersweet chocolate (60 to 70%), finely chopped

1⅔ cups (400 ml) heavy cream

2 tbsp (28 g) unsalted butter, cubed, at room temperature

DECORATION OPTIONS

A dusting of unsweetened cocoa powder, fresh berries, a sprinkling of cocoa nibs or flaky salt for a bit of crunch, a drizzle of melted chocolate or caramel such as Molly's Favorite Salted Caramel Sauce (page 159) or chopped toasted nuts

Line a 9½-inch (24-cm) tart pan or six individual 4-inch (10-cm) tins with the pâte sucrée dough. Blind bake it and allow to cool completely. Unmold it and place on your serving platter.

Place the finely chopped chocolate in a medium-sized bowl. In a small saucepan, heat the cream over medium heat until it starts to simmer (watch it closely!). Pour over the chocolate, then wait a couple of minutes for the chocolate to begin to melt.

Use a whisk to stir in the center of the bowl to create an emulsion and form a ganache. Then, stir in the butter.

Immediately pour into the baked tart crust(s). If using a large tart crust, make sure it's on the plate you'll be serving it on, as the tart will be difficult to move once it is filled. Wiggle the tart shell or smooth the top with an offset spatula as needed.

Let the tart sit undisturbed at room temperature for about 3 hours, to set and firm up before serving. How long it takes depends on the temperature of the room. If you need to speed this up (or it's a really warm day), transfer it to the refrigerator to chill.

The tart should be at room temperature when served, for the best creamy interior texture. This can take some time, so take it out of the fridge 1 to 2 hours or more before serving. Decorate with your choice of the suggested garnishes, or whatever you come up with!

MAKE AHEAD

The tart can be prepared the day before. The crust will stay crisp, and the filling delicious. Decorate close to when you'll be serving it, for the best "wow" factor.

NOTES

If you're having trouble cutting the tart, warm a knife by running it under hot water and drying it each time you make a slice, for an easy clean cut.

If you have any ganache left over, the One-Bite Chocolate Truffles (page 55) are the perfect way to use it up.

CRÈME AU CITRON: NO-FUSS LEMON CURD

Tarte au citron (lemon tart) is ranked the most preferred dessert of the French. The tart is filled with lemon curd, *crème au citron,* which is a perfectly smooth custard or cream, with a zingy punch! But lemon curd isn't just for tarts; it's the perfect base to be used as a beautiful filling for French macarons, cream puffs and cakes.

Lemon curd can be made in mere minutes and requires just a little stirring on the stove. I learned it a couple of ways while working in pâtisseries. All were fast, none needed a double boiler and my favorite method doesn't even require a thermometer! Simply heat sugar, lemon juice, lemon zest and eggs together in a saucepan. Make sure to whisk constantly and remove from the heat just when it starts to boil. Mix in the cold butter, et voilà.
Then, just let it set and thicken!

Curd can be made with just about any fruit juice. The same base recipe applies. Just substitute whatever juice or puree you'd like for the lemon juice. A beautiful example is the Raspberry-Thyme Curd (page 76) used to fill macarons. For the Roasted Strawberry Curd Cream Puffs (page 68), the strawberry flavor is amplified in the oven before making the curd. Fresh herbs are added to the Lime-Basil Curd Tarts (page 71). There are so many variations to try!

BASE RECIPE: LEMON CURD

BIG BATCH: MAKES 2³/₄ CUPS (750 G)
SMALLER BATCH: MAKES 1¹/₂ CUPS (400 G)

This recipe is the perfect way to bring some sunshine to any day of the week. It's made with whole eggs, for a fresher and lighter taste. You can whip up a batch at any time to stick in the fridge to spread on toast, cookies or scones. Or make a Tarte au Citron Meringuée ou Pas! (page 71), pipe it to fill French macarons (page 75) or use it as a topping for Madeleine Cakes with Cherries (page 73). I have listed two quantities, which you'll need depending on which recipe in the book you are making.

BIG BATCH
16 tbsp (2 sticks [224 g]) unsalted butter, cold, cubed

3 large eggs

¾ cup (150 g) granulated sugar

⅔ cup (160 ml) fresh lemon juice

Zest of 2 lemons

SMALLER BATCH
11 tbsp (1 stick + 3 tbsp [150 g]) unsalted butter, cold, cubed

2 large eggs

½ cup (100 g) granulated sugar

½ cup (120 ml) fresh lemon juice

Zest of 1 lemon

Place the cold cubed butter in a large bowl and balance a large sieve on top. We'll use this to strain the curd after it's cooked, to make sure it's nice and smooth.

In a medium-sized saucepan, whisk together the eggs and sugar. Then, incorporate the lemon juice and zest. If some eggshell or lemon seeds find their way into the pan, don't worry about fishing them out, as you'll be straining the mixture.

Place the saucepan over medium heat and whisk constantly for 5 to 7 minutes (there's no walking away from this one!). The mixture will foam and then you will feel it slightly thicken. Right after this, it will start to boil. As soon as you see bubbles, remove from the heat.

NOTES

It can sometimes be difficult to see whether the mixture is boiling. After you feel it thicken, stop whisking for a couple of seconds to check.

You might be surprised that the curd doesn't look super thick at this point. That's because the setting process has just begun. It will continue to firm up as it chills in the refrigerator for several hours, until it reaches its final stage of thickness.

Two things you can do quickly (off the heat) to check to see whether it's thickened: Dip a spoon into the mixture. Make sure it coats the back, then run a finger down the middle. A defined line should remain. Or check that the temperature is between 170 and 180°F (76 and 82°C).

Pour the cooked curd into the sieve, over the butter. Push it through the sieve with a spatula by rubbing it against the mesh (don't forget to scrape the curd from the bottom of the sieve). Then, whisk together until the butter is completely melted. It will look very liquid at this point. Cover with plastic wrap, touching the curd (this will prevent a skin from forming). Chill until firm, which may take as long as 5 hours. Letting it chill overnight is best.

MAKE AHEAD
The curd is good for 1 week in the fridge or 2 to 3 months in the freezer.

ROASTED STRAWBERRY CURD CREAM PUFFS

SERVES 12

I was teaching a pastry workshop at legendary cook Kate Hill's Camont, her eighteenth-century farmhouse in Gascony. We had baskets of fragrant strawberries picked at a farm down the road; in a moment of inspiration, Kate suggested we roast them! And that afternoon, a roasted strawberry obsession was born!

Roasting strawberries concentrates their flavor, and it's beyond easy. The strawberries need to be fresh to achieve this. The color of the curd will depend on the type of strawberry and the ripeness. To finish the cream puffs, a couple of fresh strawberry slices are tucked inside, making for a nice surprise.

ROASTED STRAWBERRY PUREE

1 cup (160 g) fresh strawberries, hulled and halved or cut into big slices

1 tsp granulated sugar

2 tbsp (30 ml) water

ROASTED STRAWBERRY CURD

1 recipe Big Batch Lemon Curd (page 67), replacing the lemon juice with ¼ cup (60 ml) lemon juice plus ½ cup (120 ml) Roasted Strawberry Puree

1 recipe Cream Puffs (page 85)

CHANTILLY CREAM

1½ cups (360 ml) heavy cream

¼ cup (30 g) powdered sugar

1 tsp vanilla extract

TO DECORATE

Fresh whole or sliced strawberries (optional)

MAKE THE ROASTED STRAWBERRY PUREE

Preheat the oven to 400°F (200°C).

Place the halved or sliced fresh strawberries in a parchment-lined casserole dish. This will help contain the juices. Sprinkle with the granulated sugar and roast in the oven for 20 to 30 minutes, or until the strawberries have released some of their juices and are soft. Some berries could be a little singed around the edges.

Remove from the oven and allow to cool, then pick up the parchment and scrape the strawberries and juice into a blender. Add the water and puree until smooth. You can strain the puree, but I like to leave the little seeds and bits of pulp for a natural look.

Measure ½ cup (120 ml) for the curd. If you don't have enough, top up with lemon juice or water.

(CONTINUED)

MAKE THE ROASTED STRAWBERRY CURD

Follow the instructions for Big Batch Lemon Curd (page 67), replacing the ⅔ cup (160 ml) of lemon juice with ½ cup (120 ml) of the roasted strawberry puree plus ¼ cup (60 ml) of fresh lemon juice.

Cover with plastic wrap, touching the surface. Chill for 3 to 5 hours to set until firm.

Meanwhile, make the cream puffs. Allow them to cool completely.

MAKE THE CHANTILLY CREAM

When ready to assemble the choux: In a stand mixer fitted with the whisk attachment, or with a hand mixer, whip the heavy cream with the powdered sugar and vanilla on medium-high speed to medium-firm peaks. It should be firm enough to hold its shape when piped.

Transfer to a piping bag fitted with a large star tip (see chart, page 12).

Cut the cooked and cooled cream puffs in half horizontally, using a serrated knife. Push down any weblike dough in each lower portion to create a cavity for the curd.

Spoon or pipe the curd inside. For a special surprise, add a couple of sliced fresh strawberries on top of the curd or press a whole strawberry in the middle. Then, finish off with a swirl of Chantilly cream!

You can replace the tops of the puffs as a little hat on the Chantilly cream, or eat them!

STORAGE

Keep cream puffs chilled in the fridge for up to 2 days. Freeze any extra curd for up to 2 to 3 months, or keep in the fridge for 1 week.

MAKE AHEAD

The curd is best when made the day before or up to 7 days ahead. This allows it plenty of time to cool and set completely.

The cream puffs can be baked and frozen, or the dough frozen uncooked and then baked from frozen. Follow the make ahead tips on page 84.

NOTES

To prepare this with frozen strawberries, skip the roasting, defrost and puree with the water. Their flavor won't be as pronounced, but they will still be delicious!

The lemon juice in this recipe is equal to about 1 juicy lemon, but measure it to be sure. Lemon juice keeps the flavor bright, as often curds made with noncitrus fruits can taste gummy or a bit muted.

TARTE AU CITRON MERINGUÉE OU PAS!

✒ SERVES 6 TO 8 ✒

You can design a lemon tart in so many ways—from simple to gourmet! Often pâtisseries have two different kinds in their case: tarte au citron and tarte au citron meringuée. The French are quite opinionated about whether it's better with or without meringue, but I prefer both!

½ recipe Pâte Sucrée (page 17)
1 recipe Big Batch Lemon Curd (page 67)

TO DECORATE
Fresh berries

OR

1 recipe Italian Meringue (page 173), using 2 or 3 egg whites, depending on how high you want the topping to be

Prepare the pâte sucrée and line either a 9- to 9½-inch (23- to 24-cm) or six individual tart molds with the dough. Blind bake until golden brown. Remove from the oven and let cool at room temperature.

Meanwhile, prepare the lemon curd. Pour in the hot lemon curd (if the pastry crust is a little warm, that's okay). Jiggle slightly to even out the top and pop any bubbles with a toothpick.

Let set uncovered in the fridge for 3 to 5 hours, or until firm. Then, decorate the top with fresh berries or Italian meringue—your choice.

To decorate with the Italian meringue, use a piping bag fitted with a decorative tip, an offset spatula or simply a spoon and swirl the meringue on top. *Psst.* Use the meringue right after it's made for the smoothest finish.

To toast the meringue, use a kitchen torch or broil the tart in the oven for 1 to 2 minutes, watching closely, until the top starts to brown.

STORAGE
Keeps chilled for up to 3 days.

MAKE AHEAD

The tart can be assembled the day before (including putting the meringue on top). The meringue is best the day it is made, but will be just fine the next day, too. Make the lemon curd up to 5 days in advance and smooth it into the baked crust when ready to serve. The tart dough will last for 2 days in the fridge, or 1 month in the freezer.

VARIATION

Lime-Basil Curd Tart: Replace the lemon juice and zest with lime juice and the zest of 3 limes. Add ¼ cup (10 g) of roughly chopped fresh basil to the saucepan with the lime juice. As this will be strained out of the cooked curd, to add a speckled look, add 2 tablespoons (5 g) of finely chopped fresh basil, zest of 1 lime and a tiny bit of green food coloring (optional) at the end once the butter has been whisked in.

MADELEINE CAKES WITH CHERRIES AND LIGHT LEMON CURD TOPPING

✤ MAKES 12 INDIVIDUAL CAKES ✤

This recipe is a little combination of my American side and my love for French complexity in taste. They look a bit like cupcakes, but are filled with layers of French components. I love the idea of these being a fun interactive pastry. Dip the fresh cherries in the light lemon curd and then devour the rest of the cake. You might have a little light lemon curd left over after assembling the cakes. Place it on the table in a bowl along with the cakes and even more fresh cherries so everyone can have an extra helping.

LIGHT LEMON CURD
1 recipe Smaller Batch Lemon Curd (page 67)

1½ cups (360 ml) heavy cream

MADELEINE CAKES
10 tbsp (1 stick + 2 tbsp [140 g]) unsalted butter, cubed

2 large eggs, at room temperature

½ cup (100 g) granulated sugar

3 tbsp (45 ml) whole milk

1 tbsp (15 g) honey

Zest of 1 lemon

1 cup (125 g) all-purpose flour

1½ tsp (7 g) baking powder

TO ASSEMBLE
Baking spray or melted unsalted butter, for muffin tin

About ¼ cup (60 g) cherry jam

1 pint (275 g) fresh cherries, to decorate

Prepare the lemon curd (the heavy cream will be incorporated later), cover with plastic wrap, touching the top of the curd, and chill at least 1 hour.

For the madeleine batter, melt the butter. Let cool at room temperature.

In a big bowl, whisk together the eggs and sugar well for about 30 seconds. Then, add the milk, honey and lemon zest.

In a separate bowl, combine the flour and baking powder. Add to the egg mixture and whisk to combine. Whisk in the cooled melted butter in two additions.

At this point, the batter can be covered and chilled up to 2 days, or baked immediately.

WHEN READY TO ASSEMBLE
Preheat your oven to 350°F (175°C).

Spray a 12-well muffin tin with baking spray or brush with melted butter, then divide the madeleine batter evenly between the wells. This can be done with a large scoop, spoon or piping bag. The batter will come up about halfway in each well.

(CONTINUED)

Bake for 12 to 15 minutes, or until golden brown and slightly pulling away from the sides. Remove from the oven and let cool for 10 minutes in the tin, then turn out onto a clean kitchen towel and let cool completely. Once the cakes are cool to the touch, remove the lemon curd from the fridge to warm up slightly while you finish preparing the cakes.

Use a paring knife to cut a hole in the top of the cakes, just as if you were removing the stem from the top of a tomato. Cut at an angle in a circle to make a hole that's about the same dimension as a teaspoon-sized measuring spoon. Fill the holes with cherry jam, about 1 teaspoon per cake. This adds a fun punch of flavor!

FINISH MAKING THE LIGHT LEMON CURD

In the bowl of a stand mixer fitted with the whisk attachment or with a hand mixer, whip the heavy cream to medium-firm peak and add it to the bowl with the lemon curd. Fold the two together with a spatula until smooth. The lemon curd should still be cool, but should have warmed up enough to where it is fluid and easy to stir before you incorporate the whipped cream.

Transfer to a piping bag fitted with a decorative tip (in the photo, I used a large open star tip). Pipe in a mound on the center of each cake, leaving a cherry-width margin around the edge. Place fresh cherries on the top of the cakes, around the light lemon curd, to decorate.

Keep chilled until serving. Devour with any leftover light lemon curd cream and a big bowl of fresh cherries.

STORAGE

Store leftovers in an airtight container in the fridge for up to 2 days.

MAKE AHEAD

This is the perfect recipe to make across 2 days to divide up the work. The day before, make the madeleine cake batter and lemon curd so they can chill overnight. This makes the madeleine batter easier to handle, allows the curd plenty of time to cool and develops the flavors.

On the day you'd like to serve them, bake the cakes. While they are cooling, finish preparing the light lemon curd topping. Then, assemble and decorate!

FRENCH MACARON TOWER WITH LEMON CURD OR RASPBERRY-THYME CURD FILLING

 MAKES 20 MACARONS

My best tip for the tower is to do a test batch of macarons, plan ahead and keep in mind that macarons freeze perfectly. It's the best way to store them! This recipe makes 20 macaron shells and enough of each curd to fill 20 macarons. How many macarons you need depends on the number of people attending (count on each person eating two or three), or how full you want the tower to look. The photo includes two double batches for a total of 80 macarons. The curd recipes can be doubled just as easily as the macaron recipe. A rule of thumb is to do only one color per macaron batch, as splitting the batter into multiple colors can cause overmixing.

It's important to approach macarons as a "project cookie" that may need trying a few times to get right. Often, the recipe needs to be adjusted for your kitchen by baking them a little longer or a little less, and turning up or down the oven temperature. They are tricky to make, but that doesn't mean you can't! I've included a lot of tips in the recipe to help you out every step of the way.

Take your time, read the recipe closely before you start and look out for three M's specifically:

1. **Measure:** I highly recommend using a kitchen scale for this recipe. Very precise weighing of each ingredient (even the egg whites) means you're on the road to success.

2. **Meringue:** Most of the issues with macarons come from the meringue. Read the General Meringue Notes on page 174 and make sure you have a stiff peak before adding the dry ingredients.

3. **Macaronage:** This is the process of combining the meringue with the powdered sugar and almond flour. You are looking for a specific texture: a thick, slow ribbon falling from the spatula. After mixing in the third addition of dry ingredients, proceed very carefully. Check for this texture frequently as it can be overmixed easily. When that happens, the batter will fall from the spatula very quickly as it has gotten too thin.

(CONTINUED)

LEMON CURD
1 recipe Smaller Batch Lemon Curd (page 67)

RASPBERRY-THYME CURD
½ cup (70 g) fresh or frozen and thawed raspberries

11 tbsp (1 stick + 3 tbsp [150 g]) unsalted butter, cubed, cold

½ cup (100 g) granulated sugar

2 large eggs

Zest of 1 lemon

3 tbsp (45 ml) fresh lemon juice (usually 1 juicy lemon)

½ tsp fresh thyme leaves + more for decoration

FRENCH MACARON COOKIE BATTER
100 g egg whites (from about 3 large eggs)

100 g (½ cup) granulated sugar

135 g (1⅓ cups) almond flour

120 g (1 cup) powdered sugar

Gel or powdered food coloring

MAKE THE FILLING
Choose your curd flavor: Lemon or Raspberry-Thyme. Each curd recipe makes enough filling for 20 macaron cookies. If you want to make both curds, double your macaron cookies!

PREPARE THE LEMON CURD (IF USING)
Prepare the lemon curd and set aside.

PREPARE THE RASPBERRY-THYME CURD (IF USING)
In a blender, puree the raspberries until smooth. You should have about ¼ cup (60 ml) of puree. If needed, top up with extra lemon juice. Set aside.

Place the cubed butter in a large bowl and have a strainer nearby.

In a small to medium-sized saucepan, whisk together the granulated sugar and eggs. Then, mix in the lemon zest and juice, thyme and raspberry puree. Heat over medium heat, constantly whisking. It will foam and then start to thicken. As soon as it boils, remove from the heat.

If you see little bits of cooked egg, pour through the strainer into the cubed butter. Or you can simply just pour it into the bowl of butter. Whisk until the butter is completely melted. Cover with plastic wrap, touching the surface, and chill for several hours until firm.

MAKE THE FRENCH MACARON COOKIE BATTER
Preheat your oven to 325°F (165°C), using the convection setting, if possible. This helps move the heat around in the oven for a more even bake. The oven temperature might need to be adjusted down by 5 to 10°F (3 to 6°C), but this depends on your oven.

NOTE
To help with piping, before you begin, you can make a guide on a piece of cardboard, tracing 1½-inch (4-cm) circles on top, with about a 1-inch (2.5-cm) margin around each. This can be slid under a sheet of parchment or silicone mat so you can see the lines, then slid out from underneath once the macarons have been piped. Alternatively, you can use a silicone baking mat that was presold with circles printed on top, or just eyeball it. My preferred surface to pipe on, in any case, is silicone as it helps keep the circle shape the best.

(CONTINUED)

Place the egg whites in the bowl of a stand mixer fitted with the whisk attachment and the granulated sugar in a separate bowl nearby. Sieve together the almond flour and powdered sugar and set aside.

WHIP UP THE MERINGUE

Whisk together the egg whites on medium speed. Once the egg whites are foamy and no liquid egg white is left in the bottom of the bowl, increase the speed to medium-high and gradually start to add the granulated sugar, a small spoonful at a time. When all the sugar has been added and the egg whites are at about medium peak, add the food coloring. How much you use depends on how dark or light you want the color to be. Add a couple of drops, see whether you like the color, then add more.

Continue whipping until the egg whites feel thick and hold a stiff peak when you lift up the beater. See the photos on page 171 for a picture of the different meringue peaks for a helpful visual.

MAKE THE BATTER

Fold the sifted almond flour mixture into the meringue in thirds, mixing until the batter falls from the spatula in a thick ribbon. Be careful to not overmix, as this will often cause the macarons to be flat and not develop a ruffly foot around the edge. Check for this texture frequently after adding the last third of the dry ingredients. The batter will become smoother the more you fold and deflate the meringue until it flows a little like lava in the bowl. Then, when you pick up a big scoop, turning your spatula to the side, it will fall slowly in a thick ribbon.

Transfer to a piping bag fitted with a large round piping tip (8 to 10 mm; see chart, page 12).

Line a baking sheet with parchment paper or a silicone mat and slip the marked cardboard guide underneath, if using. Or use a silicone mat where the circles are printed on top, or simply eyeball it. To keep the parchment paper from sliding, carefully dot a small amount of batter in the corners of the baking sheets to "glue" the paper down.

PIPE THE MACARONS

Pipe with the nozzle perpendicular and about ¼ inch (6 mm) from the baking sheet. Press until the batter reaches the edge of the circle marking. Stop applying pressure and use the tip to swirl and cut off the batter, helping to prevent a point from forming.

NOTES

To eyeball the diameter as you pipe, remember that all you need are 2 macarons of the same size to pair up and sandwich together with the filling.

Pipe the first macaron to the size you want and then when you pipe the next one, keep an eye on the size of the first. See page 12 for even more piping tips.

After you've piped one tray, wait to pipe the remaining macarons until the first baking sheet is in the oven. The batter will be fine at room temperature in the piping bag while you wait.

PREPARE AND BAKE THE MACARONS

Tap the bottom of the baking sheet several times. I hold one side of the pan and hit the bottom with the palm of my other hand, then switch to make sure both sides are done. This brings out air bubbles and flattens the tops.

Let sit for 15 minutes at room temperature. Then bake, on the middle rack, setting your oven timer to 12 minutes. It helps to open the oven door every once in a while to release steam as they are baking.

Check them with the "wiggle test" when the timer goes off at 12 minutes by opening the oven and touching the top of one of the macarons. Try to gently wiggle it. If it moves, the inside isn't done and they need to bake for a minute or two longer. If the top doesn't move, then they are baked through and the inside is fully set. When in doubt, bake them for a minute longer, as you won't be able to put them back in the oven if you discover later that they aren't baked through.

Remove from the oven and let cool completely on the baking sheets before removing from the parchment or baking mat. Macarons need to be filled on the day they are made, or the shells will dry out.

FILL THE MACARONS

Line up the macaron shells, matching each with a mate of the same size. Place one of the shells with the bottom facing up (see picture 1) for easy filling. Transfer your filling to a piping bag fitted with a large round tip (8 to 10 mm; see chart, page 12) or cut a large opening in the bag. Pipe a grape-sized amount of curd on each half that is facing up. Carefully cradle the shell, the piped filling up, in the palm of your hand and sandwich the other shell on top (see picture 2), using multiple fingers to wiggle and press down. These are fragile cookies and the shells will break if you press them together on a hard surface.

ASSEMBLE THE TOWER

Defrost any frozen macarons in the fridge overnight (see Make Ahead). Stack a smaller cake stand on top of a larger one, for height. Then, arrange your macarons as you'd like!

MAKE AHEAD

Keep filled macarons in an airtight container in the fridge for 3 days or in the freezer for 1 month.

NOTE

You can make macarons on a humid day! Make sure all your doors and windows are closed. Turn on the oven 15 minutes before baking, to help burn off humidity in the air, and bake the macarons for a minute or two longer.

PÂTE À CHOUX: THE MULTIPURPOSE DOUGH!

Could there be anything more French than pâte à choux? Or more versatile? It's a unique dough made in a saucepan. The signature feature is the hollow center that forms when baked. It is perfect to fill with pastry cream, jam, curd or even ice cream, which makes it quite the multipurpose dough! It's used to make everything from irresistible Cream Puffs and Éclairs (page 85) to Profiteroles covered in a decadent chocolate sauce (page 93) to bite-sized Chouquettes (page 90). Even the fabulous Berry Paris-Brest (page 94), a cake made to celebrate a bike race, is made with a big ring of pâte à choux!

The baking method might be a bit different from what you are used to, but it's very easy, essentially a bit of cooking on the stove and stirring in eggs. The hollow center is formed when the dough is heated in the oven. The large quantity of liquid in the batter evaporates and produces steam. This expands the dough, making it rise and filling the inside with lovely weblike threads and holes.

One of Catherine de Médicis's chefs brought the recipe for pâte à choux from Italy in 1540, when Catherine came to France to marry King Henry II. After several name changes, pastry chefs settled on pâte à choux in the eighteenth century, as the puffs made from the dough reminded them of little choux (cabbages)! So, let's go make some tasty puffs, which are much more delicious than a baked cabbage.

BASE RECIPE: PÂTE À CHOUX

❧ MAKES 2¹/₄ CUPS (600 G) ❧

When you apply for a job in a pastry shop, you have a trial day, when the chef asks you to make several recipes. New hires are often asked to bake pâte à choux, since the recipe requires a little arm muscle (when made entirely by hand) and an eye for certain textures. At one bakery, I did a trial where the quantity of pâte à choux dough turned out to be about five times more than this recipe. There was a lot of teeth gritting, but I got the job!

It is a fantastic dough to master as it is used to make so many different French recipes. The keys to pâte à choux: looking for the right texture to know that enough egg has been added, and not opening the oven during the baking process!

½ cup (120 ml) water
½ cup (120 ml) whole milk
7 tbsp (100 g) unsalted butter, at room temperature, cut into small cubes
1 tsp granulated sugar
½ tsp salt
1¼ cups (150 g) all-purpose flour
3 to 5 large eggs

Preheat your oven as noted in the recipe you're making. It will vary according to the shape and size of the desired product.

In a small to medium-sized saucepan, combine the water, milk, butter, sugar and salt. It's important that the butter is at room temperature and cut into small cubes so the liquid doesn't boil for a long time while it melts. This can cause too much water to evaporate and can affect the final texture.

Measure the flour and have it nearby. Heat the liquid ingredients over medium heat, stirring as needed, until they come to a full boil and the butter is melted. Turn off the heat as soon as a full boil is reached.

Add the flour all at once. Stir with a wooden or heatproof spoon until a ball of dough forms. Turn the heat back on to medium and stir continuously for 30 seconds to 1 minute, until a slight film covers the bottom of the pan. This dries out the dough a little and also cooks off any flour flavor.

NOTE
If the dough doesn't come together and looks a bit like oatmeal, this can be because the liquid wasn't at a full boil or there was a measurement error.

Transfer the dough from the saucepan to a clean large bowl (if making this by hand) or the bowl of a stand mixer fitted with a paddle attachment. Mix for several minutes on low speed until the dough is no longer steaming. Get those muscles out if you're stirring this by hand using a spoon! You can do it!

Next, mix in 3 eggs, one at a time, on low-medium speed, fully incorporating each before adding the next. The dough will look separated and then come together as you continue to mix it.

(CONTINUED)

Check the dough after you've added 3 eggs. To test, take a spoon, scoop up a large amount of dough, turn the spoon to the side and wait for the dough to fall. It will take several seconds to drop. When it is the right texture, it will fall in a defined point known as a *bec d'oiseau* (bird's beak) and look silky smooth (see picture below). Test for this several times to be sure.

The amount of eggs you need to get to this point depends on your flour and the humidity in your kitchen on any given day. If the dough is just about there, add just a little beaten egg at a time and test until you have that nice point. If it still seems very thick, it might need another full egg or two before you reach the right texture.

Pipe the dough into the desired shape for the recipe in which it is used. You can pipe it onto parchment paper or a silicone baking mat (this is not recommended though when piping éclairs). If using parchment, a helpful tip is to pipe small dots of the batter in the corners of the baking sheet to "glue" the parchment paper to the pan. This makes it a whole lot easier to pipe. With two to three wet fingers, pat down any points or help form your piped shapes into better mounds.

MAKE AHEAD
METHOD 1
Pipe and bake the dough. Remove from the oven and let cool completely, then transfer to freezer bags and freeze. When you're ready to use them, re-crisp the choux directly from frozen, baking in a preheated 375°F (190°C) oven for 2 to 3 minutes, or until hot to the touch. Keep a close eye on them as they can burn easily.

METHOD 2
Pipe the dough onto a silicone baking mat (you need that nonstick surface to easily peel them off), use a wet finger to pat down any points, freeze, then transfer to a freezer bag. Bake from frozen according to the same baking times and temperatures as called for in the recipe.

NOTES ON BAKING
DO NOT OPEN the oven when the dough is baking until it is deep golden brown. This dough is dependent on the steam created from the liquid content and the heat that expands and stretches the dough into beautiful hollow shapes just waiting to be filled or eaten as is!

Bake to the recommended time or until a deep golden brown to ensure it has enough of a structure to stay upright or it's possible that it will deflate. To test, open the oven, reach inside and carefully pick up and drop one of the choux. It should feel surprisingly light. If it doesn't, bake for another couple of minutes and then test again. It's better to err on the side of baking longer.

If your oven doesn't have a window, peek inside quickly to check for the color at the end of the baking time before opening the oven fully.

CREAM PUFFS AND ÉCLAIRS

❧ MAKES ABOUT 12 CREAM PUFFS AND 24 ÉCLAIRS ❧

You can have so much fun making cream puffs and éclairs! The base is the same; they're just different shapes! Fill them with whatever you'd like: Imagine combining jams, curds or fresh fruit all in one puff. Then, decorate the top with a glaze, a big dollop of whipped cream or crisp caramel! I've included four variations (vanilla, chocolate, lemon and mixed berry) and added suggestions for even more. Expect each person to eat one or two. If you have leftover dough, you can freeze it (following the make ahead instructions in the Pâte à Choux recipe (page 84), or make Chouquettes (page 90).

1 recipe Pâte à Choux (page 83)

Preheat your oven to 375°F (190°C). Prepare the pâte à choux dough. Line a baking sheet with a sheet of parchment (does not work well with Silpat). Dab dough in the corners of the baking sheet to "glue" down the paper, to make it easier to pipe. If you'd like, you can use a silicone baking mat for cream puffs, but not for éclairs as it will cause the bottoms of éclairs to concave.

TO PIPE CREAM PUFFS

Fill a pastry bag fitted with a 12-mm round piping tip (see chart, page 12) with the pâte à choux dough. Hold the pastry bag perpendicular about 1 inch (2.5 cm) above the prepared baking sheet. Press to form a tall mound 2 to 2¼ inches (5 to 6 cm) in diameter and 1 inch (2.5 cm) tall.

When it's the right size, release the pressure, swirling on the top using the tip to cut off any points. I suggest piping one choux, measuring to see whether it's about right and then using that as an example for the rest. If needed, you can always scrape up the dough and pipe it again.

Leave at least 2 inches (5 cm) of space around each cream puff. Pat down any tips or bumps with fingers wetted in water.

TO PIPE ÉCLAIRS

Use a 12-mm round or star tip with short prongs (see chart, page 12). Hold the pastry bag at a 45-degree angle to the baking sheet. Apply even pressure and move to form a line. When it's 5 to 5½ inches (13 to 14 cm) long, stop applying pressure and angle up and over the éclair to cut it off.

BAKE

If you have two pans to bake, it's best to use the convection oven setting. If using convection, adjust the temperature down by 25°F (10°C) and keep an eye on the pastries, as they may be done a bit earlier than noted. Remember, you can't open the oven to switch them halfway through the baking time. If one pan looks done before the other, quickly open the oven to take it out.

If using a standard oven, bake only one pan at a time. The second pan can sit at room temperature until the oven is free. Bake for 30 to 40 minutes, depending on the size of the pastries. Resist the urge to open the oven until they are a deep golden brown or have baked at least 30 minutes.

Test to see whether they are done by carefully lifting one up and dropping it. If it feels light and hollow, they are ready! If not, bake for a few more minutes. Remove from the oven and let cool completely before filling.

(CONTINUED)

TO FILL
METHOD 1

Cut the cream puffs or éclairs in half with a serrated knife, fill the base with something delicious, then top with whipped cream. Either place the bit that was cut off on top as a little hat or enjoy it as a snack!

METHOD 2

Transfer the filling to a piping bag fitted with a 5- to 6-mm round piping tip. Punch a hole in the bottom of each cream puffs, or two or three holes in the bottom of each éclair, using a kebab skewer, a chopstick or even clean kitchen shears. Press to fill, holding the choux in 1 hand and the piping bag in the other. When it feels heavy and a little bit comes out the hole, it's full! Wipe off any excess on the side of a bowl or with a clean finger.

FILLING OPTIONS

VANILLA

Fill with Vanilla Pastry Cream (page 35). Make a single batch if cutting the cream puffs or éclairs in half. Make a double batch if filling them completely. To finish, dip in a white glaze flavored with ½ teaspoon of vanilla extract or paste, caramel or a swirl of Chantilly Cream (page 89).

CHOCOLATE

Fill with the chocolate variation of Vanilla Pastry Cream (page 36). Make a single batch if cutting the cream puffs or éclairs in half. Make a double batch if filling them completely. To finish, drizzle or dip in melted chocolate, or sprinkle with cocoa nibs, chocolate sprinkles or shavings. Swirl Chantilly Cream (page 89) flavored with 2 to 3 tablespoons (10 to 15 g) of unsweetened cocoa powder. *See photo on page 87.

LEMON

Fill with Smaller Batch Lemon Curd (page 67). Finish with Italian Meringue (page 173, the recipe with 2 egg whites), Chantilly Cream (page 89) or a yellow glaze.

MIXED BERRY

Fill with Vanilla Pastry Cream (page 35), Smaller Batch Lemon Curd (page 67) or the Raspberry-Thyme Curd (page 76). Finish with Chantilly Cream (page 89), a red glaze or fresh berries. *See photo on front cover.

OTHER FILLINGS TO CONSIDER

Lime-Basil Curd (page 71), or Simple Raspberry Mousse (page 134).

(CONTINUED)

DECORATING OPTIONS

GLAZE (ROYAL ICING)

2 large egg whites (~60 g)
2½ cups (300 g) powdered sugar
Food coloring

In a bowl, whisk together the egg whites and powdered sugar. Add the desired amount of food coloring. You can always divide this into multiple bowls to make different colors. Check the consistency by touching the back of a spoon to the glaze. It should form a nice thick coating. If it seems too runny, add a little more powdered sugar. Depending on the amount of food coloring or flavorings added, this will need to be adjusted.

To coat the choux, dip and then let the excess drizzle off. Scrape off any big blobs of glaze delicately on the side of the bowl or with a clean finger, or these will drip down the sides. Turn so the glaze is facing up and clean up the edges with a clean finger. Wait to see how the glaze stays on the first one you dipped to see whether you need to adjust the glaze further.

TIP

Royal icing will dry out, creating a crust on top fairly quickly. Cover with plastic wrap or a damp paper towel until ready to use.

CHANTILLY CREAM

1½ cups (360 ml) heavy cream, cold
¼ cup (30 g) powdered sugar
1 tsp vanilla extract

In the bowl of a stand mixer fitted with the whisk attachment or with a hand mixer, whip all the ingredients together at medium-high speed until the mixture is at medium-firm peak. Transfer to a piping bag fitted with a fun tip, or simply spoon it on top!

HARD CARAMEL COATING

⅓ cup (80 ml) water
1 cup (200 g) granulated sugar

Pour the water into a small saucepan, followed by the granulated sugar. Heat over medium heat, not stirring, until the sugar begins to change color. Swirl gently, if needed at this point, to redistribute the heat. Once the mixture is light to medium amber, remove from the heat and prop up the pan on a tea towel, angling the hot caramel inside to give you more depth. This will help you to easily dip the filled cream puffs or éclairs. Use immediately.

To reheat, place over low heat and allow the caramel to slowly re-melt. Make more caramel as needed. See caramel tips on page 159.

STORAGE

Cream puffs and èclairs will keep for 2 days. Keep chilled until ready to eat.

MAKE AHEAD

Follow the make ahead instructions for the specific components. For example, pastry cream can be made 3 to 5 days in advance.

CHOUQUETTES

✥ MAKES ABOUT 40 ✥

When I pop into my favorite boulangerie for a snack, I know I'll probably leave with a bag of chouquettes. Sold by weight, a bag of these disappears before I know it! They are light, one-bite sugar-covered clouds in big pearls of crunchy sugar. On a trip to the village of Clairefontaine-en-Yvelines outside Versailles, I visited Le Hérrison, a bakery adorably named after the hedgehog. The pastry chef filled chouquettes with whipped cream and dusted them with powdered sugar, for a very decadent twist.

It might seem like this recipe makes a lot, but trust me, they'll vanish in a flash.

1 recipe Pâte à Choux (page 83)
Pearl sugar

Preheat your oven to 375°F (190°C).

Prepare the pâte à choux dough.

On a baking sheet lined with parchment paper or a silicone baking mat, pipe small mounds of pâte à choux dough, about 1½ inches (4 cm) in diameter (or whatever size you like; these are yours to enjoy, after all!), leaving at least 1 to 2 inches (2.5 to 5 cm) of space around each.

Sprinkle with the pearl sugar. You want a fairly good coating, as these will puff up as they bake, separating the pearl sugar on the finished puff. (No need to egg wash or brush water on top before adding the pearl sugar.)

Bake for 28 to 30 minutes. Remember to not open the oven until they have baked for at least 28 minutes. Opening the oven early can release steam and can cause them to deflate. Resist the urge! Wait until the chouquettes are medium to dark brown, then open the oven and test to see whether they are done. Carefully lift one up and drop it. If it feels light and hollow, they are ready! If not, bake for a few more minutes.

STORAGE
Enjoy these the day they are made!

PROFITEROLES

❧ SERVES 6 TO 8 ❧

This is a classic on French brasserie dessert menus: choux puffs, filled with a scoop of vanilla ice cream and covered with hot chocolate sauce! I like to make this recipe for a dinner party as, wow, will the guests be impressed!! Bake two or three small choux per person and have that chocolate sauce warm and ready! Then all that's left is to scoop the ice cream.

1 recipe Pâte à Choux (page 83)
1 recipe Chocolate Sauce for All Occasions (page 49)
Vanilla ice cream

Preheat your oven to 375°F (190°C).

Make the pâte à choux dough.

Prepare two baking sheets by lining them with a sheet of parchment or a silicone baking mat.

Pipe 12 to 15 mounds of dough 1½ to 2 inches (4 to 5 cm) in diameter, using a pastry bag fitted with a 10- to 12-mm round piping tip (see chart, page 12). Hold the pastry bag perpendicular about 1 inch (2.5 cm) above the baking sheet. Press to form the mound. When it's the right size, release the pressure, swirling on the top to cut it off. Leave about 2 inches (5 cm) of space around each mound. Pat down any tips or bumps with fingers dipped in water.

Bake for 30 to 40 minutes, depending on the size.

Resist the urge to open the oven to peek while they are baking. Instead, wait until the puffs are dark brown or have baked for at least 30 minutes.

Test to see whether they are done by carefully lifting one up and dropping it. If it feels light and hollow, then they are ready! If not, bake for a few more minutes until this point is reached. Remove from the oven and let cool completely.

Meanwhile, make the chocolate sauce.

Cut the cooled choux in half horizontally with a serrated knife and fill with a scoop of ice cream. Pat the top back on. Freeze until ready to eat or serve immediately with the warm chocolate sauce.

They can be served individually, portioned with two or three choux per plate, or in a big pile with the chocolate sauce poured over the top for guests to pull from.

If needed, reheat the chocolate sauce in a microwave, or in a small saucepan over the lowest heat, stirring constantly. It won't take much!

MAKE AHEAD

Follow the make ahead instructions for pâte à choux (page 84). Make and freeze the choux puffs in advance as a party time saver—you can even freeze them with the ice cream scooped inside!

NOTE

If you think your guests will use a lot of chocolate sauce, make a double batch. It's never a bad thing to have extra!

BERRY PARIS-BREST

❧ SERVES 6 TO 8 ❧

Now a constant staple in French pâtisseries, this cake was invented in 1910 to commemorate the 1,200-kilometer bike race between the towns of Paris and Brest. The base is made by piping circles of pâte à choux dough that, once baked, meld together and puff into the shape of a bike wheel. I made a summery version with fresh raspberries to flavor the cream. I have to admit, I think I like it better than the original and it's much easier to make!

I also baked another thinner ring of choux pastry to tuck inside, hidden by mounds of mousseline cream. This is completely optional, but as you'll have extra pâte à choux dough to use, I would definitely suggest it. Many pastry chefs add this to their Paris-Brest for extra height and a little lightness. Normally the inner ring is empty, but I filled it with blackberry jam for a punch of flavor in the center. I've included instructions for the simplest version without the inner ring, and how you can take it to the next level by adding the "Berry Ring" inside.

1 recipe Vanilla Pastry Cream (page 35)

1 recipe Pâte à Choux (page 83)

Baking spray, for pan

1 large egg, beaten to make an egg wash

¼ cup (30 g) sliced raw almonds

MOUSSELINE CREAM

17 tbsp (2 sticks + 1 tbsp [240 g]) unsalted butter, cubed, at room temperature—should be soft

1 cup (4 oz [125 g]) fresh raspberries, divided

TO FINISH

About ¼ cup (80 g) smooth blackberry jam (optional)

Fresh blackberries, to decorate (optional)

Powdered sugar (optional)

Make the vanilla pastry cream. Cover with plastic wrap, touching the top of the pastry cream, and chill completely, about 1 hour.

Next, prepare the pâte à choux dough.

Preheat your oven to 350°F (175°C).

Transfer the dough to a pastry bag fitted with a large round tip (12 mm), or cut off the end of a disposable pastry bag to the equivalent size (see chart, page 12). Try not to use a piping tip that's larger than this, or the base will end up being a bit too big.

To form the structure of the cake, we'll pipe 3 touching circles of dough. These will meld together as they bake to form a big ring that will be cut in half and filled with cream!

(CONTINUED)

PIPE THE BASE (SEE PICTURE BELOW)

For a little help in the circle-piping department: Piping the three rings inside an 8-inch (20-cm) round cake pan is a genius way to force it to keep its shape! Prepare the pan by spraying it with baking spray and pressing a circle of parchment onto the bottom.

If you are feeling like a circle-piping pro: Trace an 8-inch (20-cm) circle, using a cake pan as a guide, on a piece of parchment paper. Flip over and "glue" to the baking sheet by dabbing dough in the corners and pressing the paper on top.

As you pipe, hold the tip 2 inches (5 cm) above the paper and let the dough drop to the surface as you guide it, so it keeps its tall, round shape (the same size as the hole of the piping tip). Pipe the first circle of dough inside the circle you traced or the edge of the pan. Pipe another concentric circle inside the first. It should be right next to and touching the first ring. Then, on top, pipe another circle in the middle of the two you just piped.

Delicately brush the whole surface with egg wash. Then, sprinkle liberally with sliced almonds.

Bake on the middle rack for 45 to 50 minutes, or until deep golden brown. Remember to not open the oven until it is a deep golden shade or has baked for at least 45 minutes, or it might deflate.

Otherwise, pipe some little puffs or Chouquettes (page 90) on the sheet as an additional treat. They'll be able to bake at the same time as the ring.

Once the base is done, bake the single ring and/or puffs for 25 to 30 minutes, or until a deep golden brown. Let cool completely at room temperature.

PREPARE THE MOUSSELINE CREAM

Take the pastry cream out of the fridge. By hand, give it a good whisk for a nice smooth texture. Set aside.

In the bowl of a stand mixer fitted with the whisk attachment, or in a big bowl, using a handheld electric mixer, whip the soft butter for several minutes until smooth with a texture like mayonnaise.

Slowly add the pastry cream to the butter, a small spoonful at a time, while whipping on medium-high speed. Wait for each addition to be fully incorporated before adding the next. As it's hard to see, simply count to ten after each addition before plopping in the next. Scrape down the bowl a couple of times throughout.

Once all of the pastry cream is incorporated, toss in about ¾ cup (90 g) of the fresh raspberries, reserving the rest for decoration. Whip for several minutes on high speed for the mixture to come together and fluff up a bit more.

BERRY RING OPTION

While the base of the cake is baking, with the remaining dough, pipe the optional ring of pâte à choux that will be hidden on the inside of the Paris-Brest. Draw a circle, using an 8-inch (20-cm) round cake pan as a guide, on a piece of parchment. Dot the pâte à choux dough in the corners of the baking sheet, flip the parchment paper so the pencil marks are face down and then press the paper onto the dots to secure it in place. Pipe a ring just inside of the penciled circle to have approximately the right size ring to fit inside the cake.

If it looks separated, whip at a higher speed for longer (or see Notes).

ASSEMBLE THE CAKE

Transfer the raspberry mousseline cream to a piping bag fitted with a large star tip. If the cream seems very soft, chill it for 5 to 10 minutes before using it. Don't chill it for too long, or it will become solid (because of all the butter).

Cut the base of the cake in half with a serrated knife. Carefully remove and set aside the top portion, spreading your fingers wide to support it.

If you didn't make the inside ring, swirl the mousseline cream on the base and place the cut piece of cake on top.

IF YOU MADE THE BERRY RING

Fill the ring with blackberry jam: Poke holes in the ring every couple of inches to access the hollow center, using a chopstick, a kebab skewer or even the end of a pair of kitchen shears. Spoon the jam into a small disposable piping bag and cut a little off the end or use a nondisposable bag fitted with a small round piping tip large enough for the jam to flow through. Insert the tip into the holes at an angle and press to fill.

Pipe a single layer of mousseline cream inside the base of the cake for the ring to rest on and then place it on top (if the ring is too big or too small, cut and bend to adjust). Decorate around the ring with the mousseline cream. Pipe any remaining cream on top for even more height. Then, carefully position the crowning piece of choux pastry on top!

TO DECORATE

Decorate by pressing the reserved fresh raspberries and a couple of blackberries (if using) into the cream if you'd like, or leave it as is. Another option is to dust the top with powdered sugar just before serving.

Chill for at least 45 minutes to firm up the mousseline cream.

Remove from the fridge an hour before eating. The butter in the cream will be very hard and will need time to warm up before you cut yourself a big slice.

Best the day it's made, but will be good the next day, too.

MAKE AHEAD

Prepare the pastry cream up to 3 to 5 days in advance.

NOTES

It is very important that the butter for the mousseline cream is very soft. How long you need to leave it out at room temperature depends on your kitchen.

If your mousseline cream does not come together, then this is a temperature issue, usually meaning that the butter was too cold. Fan a kitchen torch back and forth briefly on the side of the bowl while whipping. You can also take out about ¼ cup (60 ml) of the batter and melt it completely in a microwave or small saucepan. Add it slowly back in while whipping to bring it together.

For a punchier pink mousseline cream, add a tiny touch of red food coloring to the bowl as you are whipping it up.

CROQUEMBOUCHE

⤜ SERVES 8 TO 10 ⤛

Also called the *pièce montée* (literally, "mounted piece"), or should I say pièce de résistance, the croquembouche is the traditional French wedding cake. It's a tower of cream puffs pieced together with liquid gold caramel. This cake is ethereal, meaning it only lasts a day, and is absolutely breathtaking. It is my favorite French dessert to make. I love the heart-pumping excitement as you work quickly to dip each choux in caramel and play a game of Tetris to fit them all together.

This recipe serves eight to ten people, assuming each person will eat two or three puffs. It can easily be doubled or tripled. As this cannot be assembled in advance, I suggest preparing the parts of the recipe ahead so you're ready when the time comes. Now, how do you eat it? Well, at a French wedding, sometimes a saber comes out to cut through hardened caramel, or a serrated knife is used. It's not pretty, but it certainly is fun!

CREAM PUFFS
2 recipes Vanilla Pastry Cream (page 35), or flavor variation of choice

1 recipe Pâte à Choux (page 83)

½ cup (120 ml) heavy cream, cold

CARAMEL
1 cup (240 ml) water

2 cups (400 g) granulated sugar

MAKE AND FILL THE CHOUX

Make the double batch of the pastry cream. Cover with plastic wrap, touching the pastry cream, and chill completely, 1 to 2 hours.

Prepare the pâte à choux dough.

Preheat your oven to 375°F (190°C). Line 2 baking sheets with parchment paper or silicone baking mats.

Transfer the dough to a piping bag fitted with a large round 10-mm tip (see chart, page 12) and pipe walnut-sized mounds (about a 1-inch [2.5-cm] diameter) on the prepared baking sheets, leaving a 1½-inch (4-cm) space around each. You'll need between 30 and 35 mounds for the croquembouche; if you have fewer or more, though, it's easy to adjust during construction.

Pat any tips down with a wet finger. Bake for 25 to 30 minutes, not opening the oven until you see they are a deep golden brown. Test for doneness by picking one up and dropping it. It should feel light and hollow. Remove from the oven and let cool completely.

In the bowl of a stand mixer fitted with the whisk attachment, whip the heavy cream to medium-firm peak.

Whisk the prepared pastry cream by hand for a smooth texture, then whisk in the whipped cream. Transfer to a piping bag with a small round (5- to 6-mm) opening (see chart, page 12).

(CONTINUED)

Arrange the choux in rows on a piece of parchment or a silicone mat on your work surface to give you a bit of a plan for how you'll construct the tower. Start at the top with two choux, then work your way down, removing one choux from each row—two, three, four, five, six, seven, . . . Set aside several choux just in case you need them to close a gap at the top or to add one to a row.

Fill the choux with the lightened pastry cream.

Use a chopstick or other utensil to pierce the flat back of each choux, leaving them in their row formation. Pick each one up and fill with lightened pastry cream until a tiny bit comes out the hole (see picture 1 on page 101). Scrape this on the side of a bowl or wipe away with a clean finger.

ONCE ALL THE CHOUX ARE FILLED, MAKE THE CARAMEL

Pour the water into a small saucepan, then add the sugar (no need to stir if the sugar is in a mound. It will dissolve as it is heated). Heat over medium heat until the mixture boils and starts to change color (no stirring!). Once it starts to change color, you can gently swirl the pan if you need to redistribute the heat.

Cook to a medium amber (it will continue to darken slightly after you turn off the heat).

Remove from the heat and prop up the pan on a tea towel so the caramel is angled and pooling at one side of the pan. Wait for the bubbles to subside, then carefully dip each of the choux, holding them at the base with your fingertips (see picture 2 on page 101).

Once dipped, swirl to contain any drips, or wipe on the side of the pan. Carefully place each back in its row with the caramel facing up.

Work fast! If you need to, reheat the caramel on the lowest heat setting (not stirring, only swirling as needed) or make a fresh batch. *Psst.* If you accidentally get caramel on you, immediately wipe it off on your apron or a towel nearby. See page 159 for even more tips!

ASSEMBLE THE CROQUEMBOUCHE

On a plate, gold board or other serving surface, plot out the lowest circle. It will be about 7 inches (18 cm) in diameter, measuring from the outside of the choux. This will vary drastically, though, depending on the size of your choux. To get an even better idea, I place the first row in a circle and hold them up, with some help from a friend, to confirm the diameter of the bottom row.

NOTE

Normally I assemble this freestyle, but you can make a cone from parchment paper to put in the middle to guide your tower. Each row should be set slightly in toward the middle, and slightly leaned toward the center so as to create a dome. Other ways to assemble follow the recipe directions.

Dip the side of each choux in caramel and stick to the base to form the first circle. For the following rows, you'll need to dip the side and a little more to either the left or right to stick the choux to the choux below, and the one next to it.

Keep working your way up, pulling and replacing from other rows as needed to make sure they fit.

At the top, angle two choux to finish it off. But see what works! Sometimes it's only one! Sometimes, it's a trifecta of three. If by chance your planning was a little off and you run out of choux, not all is lost! Oui, you can of course make more choux, but what I would suggest is filling that hole with edible flowers. You can also get creative and leave the top open on purpose to fill with something else, too, such as a lightweight Marie Antoinette porcelain figurine.

OPTIONAL SPUN SUGAR

Getting threads of sugar happens when the caramel is at a certain temperature (295 to 310°F [146 to 155°C]). You can cook a new batch of caramel and let it cool to this temperature, then dip a fork and carefully work the thread around the finished croquembouche. Or keep an eye on the caramel you are using to assemble, because as it cools and thickens, it will reach this state as well.

ASSEMBLY METHODS

For an easy, noncaramel method, attach each puff to a Styrofoam cone with a toothpick or lollipop stick that's been cut in half.

Even easier, and a favorite of mine, is a rustic approach. Simply stack the filled cream puffs in a beautiful pile!

MAKE AHEAD

This dessert only lasts for 1 day once assembled. Prepare the pastry cream 3 to 5 days in advance. Follow the make ahead tips on page 84 for the pâte à choux.

NOTE

Traditionally the choux are dipped in caramel, but there are other options:

- Bake some (or all!) of the choux with pearl sugar on top.

- Dip in a glaze (page 89), melted chocolate or melted fondant.

GÉNOISE ET JOCONDE: ROLLED OR LAYERED SPONGE CAKE

Sponge cakes are the perfect base for layered cakes, such as the Coconut-Peach Génoise Cake (page 108) and rolled cakes, such as the traditional Bûche de Noël (page 118). As their name suggests, they soak up flavored syrups like a sponge! This chapter includes two sponge cake base recipes: génoise and Joconde. They can be used interchangeably, but in French pâtisserie, the Joconde is most classically used just for the Opéra Cake (page 111). For both, the lift comes from whipping the eggs and then carefully folding in the dry ingredients, making for a lovely light spongy cake, not to be confused with a rich butter cake.

The big differences between the two recipes are (a) how the eggs are beaten and (b) the addition of almond flour in the Joconde batter. For the génoise, whole eggs and granulated sugar are whipped before folding in the dry ingredients. For the Joconde batter, it starts with making a meringue by beating the egg whites to a stiff peak with sugar, which is then folded into the batter.

BASE RECIPE 1: GÉNOISE SPONGE CAKE

MAKES 1 (10 X 15–INCH [25 X 38–CM]) ROLLED CAKE OR 1 (8- TO 9-INCH [20- TO 23-CM]) LAYERED CAKE

Use this recipe to make all kinds of cakes, both rolled and layered. It includes ingredients and instructions for both, as the quantities and baking times vary just slightly between the two.

ROLLED GÉNOISE CAKE

½ cup (65 g) all-purpose flour
1½ tbsp (20 g) unsalted butter
3 large eggs, at room temperature
1 large egg yolk
⅓ cup (65 g) granulated sugar

LAYERED GÉNOISE CAKE

1 cup (125 g) all-purpose flour
2 tbsp (28 g) unsalted butter
4 large eggs, at room temperature
½ cup (100 g) granulated sugar

NOTE

It is important to whip until this texture is achieved. It can take 8 to 10 minutes to get to this point, or sometimes even longer! Set a timer for 8 minutes and check. If it looks as if the eggs aren't whipping up after several minutes, your mixer speed is too low; in that case, increase the speed slightly. However, it's important to not whip fully on high speed, or else very big bubbles will be created. Instead, stick to medium-high speed, whipping for a longer time so a sturdier structure is created—this is what creates the lift in the sponge.

Prepare your baking pan per the recipe's instructions. Preheat your oven. For rolled cakes: 350°F (175°C). For layered cakes: 325°F (165°C).

Measure out the flour and set aside with a sieve or sifter nearby. Melt the butter and set aside to cool. In the bowl of a stand mixer fitted with the whisk attachment or in a large bowl, using a hand mixer, put the eggs, egg yolk (for a rolled cake) and sugar. If your eggs feel the least bit cool to the touch, place the whole uncracked egg in a bowl of warm water for several minutes before cracking.

Whip the egg mixture on medium-high speed until triple in volume, very pale yellow in color (practically white) and mousselike and thick in texture. Lift the beater to check the texture (see picture 1 on page 106). The batter should fall in a slow, thick ribbon and take a couple of seconds to disappear.

Sift the flour over the whipped eggs in two additions, gently folding after each until mostly incorporated. The trick is to keep as much air in the batter as possible. To fold, I repeat in my head, "Into the middle, out to the sides." Fold with a spatula dipping into the middle, scraping the bottom and then coming up and over the top. After each fold, turn the bowl a little. I'll scrape around the sides every once in a while, too.

Once the flour is just about incorporated, grab a spatula full of batter and add it to the cooled melted butter. Whisk well to mix the two together. This makes it much easier to blend into the batter. Pour the butter into the batter and fold carefully to combine (see photo 2 on page 106).

(CONTINUED)

TO BAKE

For a rolled cake: Pour the batter in a line down the prepared jelly-roll pan (see picture 3 below). Use an offset metal spatula to first spread the batter into the corners (see picture 4 below), and then fill in the rest of the pan. Do this quickly and aim for an even layer.

Immediately place in the preheated oven to keep the batter from deflating. Bake for 9 to 11 minutes. The cake is done when the top is lightly browned across the whole surface and is pulling away from the sides of the pan.

As soon as you remove it from the oven, cover with a damp, clean cloth. It's okay if the cloth touches the cake. This will keep the moisture in and help prevent any cracking. Allow to cool completely in the pan.

For a layered cake: Pour into the prepared pan and jiggle the pan so the top is nice and flat. Immediately bake for 30 to 35 minutes. The cake is done when the top is lightly browned and pulling away from the sides of the pan.

Leave, uncovered, at room temperature until completely cool to the touch.

BASE RECIPE 2: JOCONDE SPONGE CAKE

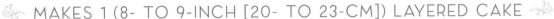

MAKES 1 (8- TO 9-INCH [20- TO 23-CM]) LAYERED CAKE

Use the extra yolks from this recipe to make Vanilla Pastry Cream (page 35) or use them for a French coffee buttercream in the Opéra Cake (page 111), the cake Joconde is most often used for.

1½ tbsp (20 g) unsalted butter
3 large egg whites (~90 g)
2 tbsp (30 g) granulated sugar
4 large eggs
1 cup (100 g) almond flour or meal
¾ cup + 1 tbsp (100 g) powdered sugar
3 tbsp (25 g) all-purpose flour

Prepare your baking pan as instructed in the recipe. Preheat your oven to 425°F (220°C).

Melt the butter in a small saucepan or a microwave and set aside.

In the bowl of a stand mixer fitted with the whisk attachment, make a French meringue by whipping the 3 egg whites on medium speed until foamy and no liquid white is left at the bottom of the bowl. Increase the speed to medium-high and gradually add the granulated sugar. Whip until the whites are at stiff peak.

Transfer the meringue to a separate bowl.

Into the mixer bowl you just used to whip the whites, crack the 4 eggs and add the almond flour, powdered sugar and all-purpose flour (no need to clean the bowl or whisk attachment).

Mix on medium speed until smooth. Then, whisk in the melted butter until completely incorporated.

Remove from the mixer and by hand, stir in one-third of the meringue to lighten the batter. Carefully fold in the remaining meringue until barely any streaks of egg whites remain. It's better to stop here than overdeflate the egg whites.

Pour into the prepared pan and bake for 10 to 12 minutes, or until springy to the touch and browned.

COCONUT-PEACH GÉNOISE CAKE

❧ SERVES 10 TO 12 ❧

Usually génoise is used for a rolled cake, as it has the flexibility and perfect texture to soak up all the flavors of the filling that's rolled inside. It can also be used for a layer cake, though! Just cut the cake in half and pile it high with whipped cream and fresh fruit.

I've done that here with peaches and cream—and a bit of coconut. Most of your time making this cake will be spent cutting peaches and assembling. The rest is simply sitting back and enjoying a massive slice of summer perfection.

Unsalted butter, for pan

All-purpose flour, for dusting

1 recipe Layered Génoise Cake (page 105), to which you will replace ¼ cup (30 g) of the all-purpose flour with ¼ cup (25 g) of unsweetened shredded coconut, and add ¼ tsp coconut extract (see directions)

PEACH SYRUP

½ cup (120 ml) water

¼ cup (50 g) granulated sugar

4 slices fresh peach, cubed

TO ASSEMBLE

4 fresh yellow peaches (1½ lb [675 g])

2 cups (1 pint [480 ml]) heavy cream, cold

½ cup (60 g) powdered sugar + more for dusting

1 tsp vanilla extract

Optional: a sprinkle of large coconut flakes, or ground cinnamon

Prepare an 8-inch (20-cm) round cake pan. You won't have a lot of time to put this in the oven once the batter comes together, so make sure to have this ready! Butter the pan (all the way up the sides), place a circle of parchment paper on the bottom and butter this. Flour the whole inside and tap off any excess.

Follow the instructions for the layered génoise cake. When you are ready to add the dry ingredients to the whipped eggs, sift in just ¾ cup (95 g) of flour and then add the shredded coconut. There's no need to sift the coconut.

Add the coconut extract to the batter at the end, with the butter.

WHILE THE CAKE BAKES, MAKE THE PEACH SYRUP

In a small saucepan, combine all the syrup ingredients and bring to a boil over medium-high heat. Lower the heat and crush the cubed peach with a fork or potato masher. Simmer for an additional 2 to 3 minutes, then turn off the heat and let cool.

ASSEMBLE THE CAKE

Remove the cooled génoise cake from the pan, running a knife around the edge and flipping it out onto a clean surface, peeling away the parchment circle. Cut the cake in half horizontally to make two layers.

NOTE
The easiest way to do this is on a cake turntable. Use a long serrated knife to gradually cut toward the center of the cake while slowly spinning it on the turntable. Alternatively, you can also score a line all the way around and use this as a guide to make the cut.

(CONTINUED)

COCONUT-PEACH GÉNOISE CAKE

COCONUT-PEACH GÉNOISE CAKE
❧ (CONTINUED) ❧

Open up the cake on a clean surface so the cut sides are exposed. Brush with the peach syrup using a brush or a crumpled-up paper towel. This will keep the layers moist and add additional flavor, essential for a sponge cake.

Transfer the bottom layer to a serving plate, cut side up. Slice 3 of the peaches and place them on top. Start with a ring of slices around the edge, the tips just barely off the edge, each slice overlapping with the last, then fill in the center with additional slices.

In a bowl, whip the cold heavy cream, powdered sugar and vanilla to a medium-firm peak.

NOTE
I always hold back just a little unwhipped cream to fix overwhipped cream. You'll know whether you beat the cream too long if it is super thick with jagged edges. To fix this, whisk in unwhipped cream either gently by hand or using an electric mixer on the lowest speed. If it's separated and started making butter, there's no saving it, but you have freshly made butter for toast!

Fill a piping bag fitted with a large open star tip (or tip of your choice!) with the whipped cream and pipe on top of the peach layer. I like to start around the edge, and then do a swirl to fill in the middle. For this cake, I made S shapes around the edge; stars would look great, too!

Flip over the remaining cake layer so the cut side rests on the whipped cream. Dust the top with powdered sugar, then decorate with the rest of the whipped cream.

Cut the last peach into slices to decorate the top and chill until serving. The peaches on top will dry out a little as they sit, so for the freshest slices, cut and decorate up to an hour before serving.

For a finishing touch, sprinkle the whipped cream on top with a pinch of cinnamon or big toasted coconut flakes (toast in a single layer in an ungreased saucepan over low heat or in a preheated 350°F [175°C] oven until the edges start to brown, 5 to 10 minutes).

MAKE AHEAD
Bake the coconut génoise cake the day before. Let cool in the pan until room temperature and then cover the top with plastic wrap. When ready to use, release from the pan by running a knife around the edge and flipping the cake onto a clean surface.

The peach syrup can be made 3 days in advance. Keep in the fridge in an airtight container.

OPÉRA CAKE

MAKES 8 INDIVIDUAL SERVINGS OR
16 TWO-BITE DESSERT HORS D'OEUVRE SERVINGS

Just like the Palais Garnier in Paris, this cake has it all: layers of coffee buttercream, chocolate ganache and Joconde cake dabbed with coffee syrup. It's even thought to have been invented to keep opera spectators awake with its high coffee and chocolate content! Now, don't be dissuaded by the long instructions. Each component is easy to do. (I've just packed in lots of tips to help you along!) Take your time and enjoy the read, because at the end of your baking adventure is a gorgeous cake that looks like the layers of balconies inside of the Opéra Garnier!

Baking spray, for pans

1 recipe Joconde Sponge Cake (page 107), reserving the egg yolks for the coffee buttercream

COFFEE SYRUP
½ cup (120 ml) water

⅓ cup (65 g) granulated sugar

1 tbsp (6 g) instant espresso powder, or 1 oz (30 ml) brewed espresso

FRENCH COFFEE BUTTERCREAM
4 large egg yolks (~60 g)

½ cup (100 g) granulated sugar

¼ cup (60 ml) water

10 tbsp (1 stick + 2 tbsp [140 g]) unsalted butter, cubed (very soft)

1 tbsp (6 g) instant espresso powder

1 tsp hot water

CHOCOLATE GANACHE
4 oz (115 g) semisweet, bittersweet or dark chocolate (60 to 70%), chopped

¼ cup (60 ml) heavy cream

1 tbsp (15 g) unsalted butter, at room temperature

CHOCOLATE GLAZE
6 oz (170 g) semisweet, bittersweet or dark chocolate (60 to 70%), chopped

¼ cup (60 ml) vegetable or coconut oil

1 tbsp (15 g) unsalted butter, at room temperature

Melted chocolate (optional)

Gold luster dust, for sprinkling (optional)

Preheat your oven to 425°F (220°C). If you haven't done so already, take out the butter for the coffee buttercream. It needs to be very soft!

Prepare the baking pans for the Joconde. (See Notes for other baking pan options.)

Spray a 9 x 13-inch (23 x 33-cm) pan and 9-inch (23-cm) square pan with baking spray and press a piece of parchment inside. Smooth the paper as flat as possible and press along the sides and in the corners. Do not spray on top of the parchment. We actually want it to stick to the cake!

MAKE THE JOCONDE BATTER
Pour one-third of the batter into the middle of the prepared 9-inch (23-cm) square baking pan. Pour the remaining batter into the prepared 9 x 13-inch (23 x 33-cm) pan. Work fast and use an offset spatula to spread the batter to fill the pans.

Immediately bake for 10 to 12 minutes, reversing the pans halfway through. The cakes are done when they are light brown across the entire surface. The large pan might need an extra minute. Remove from the oven and let cool completely in the baking pans.

Meanwhile, make the fillings.

(CONTINUED)

MAKE THE COFFEE SYRUP

Bring all the syrup ingredients to a boil and then set aside to cool. Watch closely, as it can boil over with the addition of the instant espresso powder.

PREPARE THE FRENCH COFFEE BUTTERCREAM

In the bowl of a stand mixer fitted with the whisk attachment, or with a hand mixer, beat the egg yolks for several minutes on medium speed until slightly lighter in color. In a small saucepan over medium-high heat, cook the sugar and water to 244°F (118°C) to form a sugar syrup and immediately remove from the heat. Let the bubbles subside for several seconds while giving the yolks one last quick whisk. Then, avoiding hitting the whisk—aim for the gap in between the side of the bowl and the whisk—slowly pour the hot sugar syrup into the yolks while mixing on low speed.

Once all of the hot syrup has been added, increase the speed on the mixer to medium-high and whip until the bowl is cool to the touch, about 10 minutes. The egg yolks initially will look watery with the hot syrup addition, then lighten in color and thicken as the two cool and are beaten together.

Slowly add the very soft butter, one cube at a time, while whisking on medium speed.

Mix the espresso powder with the teaspoon of hot water and then add to the buttercream, whipping to combine. Keep at room temperature. If very soft, refrigerate for 10 to 15 minutes before using. Don't chill too long, though, or it will solidify because of all the butter inside.

PREPARE THE CHOCOLATE GANACHE

Melt the chocolate in a microwave, stirring after each blast. Alternatively, melt in a double boiler, placing the chocolate in a heatproof bowl over simmering water. Heat the cream in a separate saucepan until simmering, then pour into the melted chocolate. See ganache tips on page 50.

Mix briskly with a whisk until combined, then stir in the butter. Keep at room temperature. If needed, chill briefly to firm up, but keep an eye on it so it does not get too firm to spread.

ASSEMBLE THE CAKE

From bottom layer to top, here is the layout for the finished cake: JOCONDE-BUTTERCREAM-JOCONDE-GANACHE-JOCONDE-BUTTERCREAM-GLAZE.

Cut the large rectangle of cake in half with kitchen scissors to create two 9 x 6½–inch (23 x 17–cm) pieces. Keep the parchment stuck to the back of the cake pieces. Trim to the sides of the cakes so you don't have a lot of excess. This will help move the pieces when assembling. Use one of the cake pieces as a pattern to cut the remaining rectangle from the square cake. All 3 rectangles should be identical in size, so trim as needed.

Cover a baking sheet with a clean piece of parchment paper to act as your assembly area.

Flip one of the rectangles onto the clean sheet of parchment. Carefully peel off and discard the parchment (now on top). Brush the coffee syrup on top *liberally* with a pastry brush or crumpled paper towel. This is called "imbibing." You will be permeating each of the layers throughout assembly and should use all of the coffee syrup. I'll dab three times, then refill the brush with the syrup. The top of the cake pieces may even have puddles here and there—run the brush over them to help the syrup soak into the cake.

Spread half of the coffee buttercream on top in a thin layer. Turn the baking sheet as needed throughout the process to make the cake easier to ice.

(CONTINUED)

Liberally dab the top of the second layer of cake with the coffee syrup before placing on top of the buttercream-covered layer. Gently press on top and then peel off the parchment paper. Brush the top of this second cake layer liberally with the coffee syrup, then spread all of the ganache on top.

Brush the top of the third layer of cake with the coffee syrup before flipping it over to place on top of the ganache. Press down gently and peel off the parchment paper. Dab the top with the rest of the coffee syrup. Then, cover the top of this third layer with the remaining coffee buttercream. Spread the buttercream smoothly so the glaze has a nice clean finish.

Chill for at least 30 minutes.

MAKE THE GLAZE

Melt the chocolate, oil and butter together in a microwave. This can be done in a double boiler, too, stirring everything in a heatproof bowl set on top of simmering water.

Let cool for about 30 minutes at room temperature, or until neutral to the touch (not hot, not cold).

Pour over the cold cake, starting at one end and then zigzagging down the middle. I made sure there was plenty of glaze, so there's no worry that it will run out, or that you will have to spread it on top. Firmly tap the baking sheet twice, by lifting on one side and hitting it on the counter, to even off the top. Chill for at least 30 minutes. Don't worry how even the sides look, as they'll be trimmed off to reveal the finished cake!

THE FINALE

Cut off the sides by warming a big chef's knife under hot water, drying it and then pressing it into the chocolate glaze. Push down firmly so that the cake is unveiled! Enjoy the scraps as a little treat for the chef.

To cut into smaller pieces, it's worth breaking out a ruler. Make a mark on each side at the point where you want to cut it, and then connect the dots with your knife to cut. Clean the knife and run it under hot water with each cut.

Decorate by piping "Opéra" on top in your fanciest scroll with melted chocolate (or some of the glaze mixed with powdered sugar to thicken it). Sprinkle it with gold luster dust or simply leave it as is!

Keep chilled. Remove 30 minutes before serving to allow the buttercream and ganache to warm up before eating to a standing ovation.

MAKE AHEAD

This cake can be made 3 to 4 days in advance. Do not cut it until ready to serve to keep the cake from drying out.

NOTES

The directions use a 9 x 13-inch (23 x 33-cm) baking pan and 9-inch (23-cm) square baking pan. You can skip the pans completely and spread out the cake batter to the same dimensions on two parchment-lined baking sheets. The batter is thick enough to hold its shape without the sides of a cake pan. To do this, mark the dimensions in pencil on two sheets of parchment paper, then flip over the paper. Spread the batter to fill the shapes and bake per the regular instructions.

If allergic to nuts, substitute Rolled Génoise Cake (page 105) for the Joconde.

BOMBE GÂTEAU

✤ SERVES 12 TO 14 ✤

Aptly named after its cannonball shape, the *bombe gâteau* was created in 1880. It is filled with a layer of sponge cake, ice cream, mousse or a combination of all three. In Auguste Escoffier's 1903 cookbook *Le Guide Culinaire* (which is still in print!), he mentions more than 60 different bombe gâteau ice-cream cake combinations! A couple of my favorites: the Frou-Frou (vanilla and rum with candied fruits); the Josephine (coffee and pistachio); the Miss Helyette (raspberry and vanilla); and the Marquise (apricots and Champagne)! It's a wonderful opportunity to get creative with using your favorite flavors of ice cream, adding in some cookie crumbs or other fun things!

This is a very flexible cake. Pick a bowl to use as your mold for this cake that will hold enough servings for your get-together. Use this to estimate the amount of ice cream you'll need.

Ice cream or sorbet of choice
1 recipe Rolled Génoise Cake (page 105)
Optional: crushed cookies, fudge sauce, crushed meringue or macaron shells, sprinkles . . .

TO DECORATE
A dusting of unsweetened cocoa powder or a chocolate glaze

CHOCOLATE GLAZE (OPTIONAL)
9 oz (255 g) semisweet, bittersweet or dark chocolate (60 to 70%), chopped
¼ cup (60 ml) vegetable oil or coconut oil
2 tbsp (30 g) unsalted butter, at room temperature

To start softening up the ice cream or sorbet, place it in the refrigerator with a plate underneath to catch any condensation. Keep an eye on it; this usually takes about an hour for it to be soft all the way through. Using the refrigerator slowly thaws the ice cream and works better than placing it at room temperature where the sides will be melted and the inside rock hard.

Preheat your oven to 350°F (175°C).

Make the rolled génoise cake batter and pour onto a parchment-lined baking sheet.

Spread into a rough circle about an inch (2.5 cm) thick, making sure you'll have a large enough cake to cut out a piece to fit the top of the bowl you'll be using.

Bake for 9 to 10 minutes, or until lightly browned across the whole surface. Remove from the oven and let cool completely on the baking sheet.

Use your bowl to press down and twist, cutting a circle from the baked cake. Carefully peel off the parchment and set the cake aside. Any scraps can be used inside the cake as layers, or eaten as snacks.

ASSEMBLE THE CAKE
Rub water on the inside of your bowl as if you were greasing it. This will help the plastic wrap stick. Line with three or four layers of plastic wrap, pressing it against the sides. Allow for overhang to easily pull the cake out later.

Before using each flavor of ice cream, stir it to redistribute any melted parts. Scoop it into the bowl and use a spoon or spatula to spread it in your preferred pattern. I often spread mine up the sides, leaving a big hole in the center, so each layer goes inside the last.

(CONTINUED)

You could also do stacked layers, like a napoleon, with strawberry, chocolate and vanilla. Or, for a festive look, big blobs of different flavored ice cream all over the inside of the bowl. If you plan on layering, the trick is to chill each layer of ice cream for at least 30 minutes before adding the next so each is distinct.

As you assemble, don't forget to add any toppings you'd like, such as the scraps of génoise cake. I sprinkled crushed vanilla cookies into mine. Sprinkles would be a festive touch in between two light-colored layers, too.

Once the bowl is filled, press the round piece of génoise cake on top. This will become the base. Cover with plastic wrap and freeze overnight or up to several days.

When ready to serve, dip the bowl in hot water for 2 seconds. Then, try to pull out the cake. If necessary, dip again. It doesn't take much, though! If the sides look melted, return the cake to the freezer until ready to add the finishing touches.

TO FINISH

If dusting with cocoa powder, add a nice sprinkling right before eating. I like to do this quickly with the cake on a wire rack or piece of parchment, then transfer to the serving platter, to keep the final plate clean.

IF GLAZING THE CAKE

Melt the chocolate, oil and butter together, either in a microwave or in a double boiler. Stir to combine and then let cool at room temperature until tepid to the touch, about 30 minutes.

Place the frozen cake on a wire rack or perched atop a bowl that's smaller than the base. Start pouring the glaze at the top and then wind down the sides. You'll only get one go at this, so I included lots of glaze, just in case. Do this quickly so the génoise cake doesn't get too soft to move easily. Transfer to a serving platter and either serve immediately or chill. If chilling with the glaze, be aware that as it thaws, there will be condensation. Blot to remove with a paper towel.

No matter the finishing decoration, the cake will need time to warm up enough before you're able to cut into it. This depends on the size and the type of ice cream and can take between 15 and 30 minutes.

MAKE AHEAD

The beauty of an ice-cream cake is that it can be made well in advance! Once assembled, make sure it's wrapped up nicely so the génoise doesn't dry out in the freezer.

BÛCHE DE NOËL

❦ SERVES 6 ❦

The classic bûche de Noël is a génoise cake rolled up with a delicious filling inside. Then, it's iced with ganache or buttercream and decorated to look like a log! The bûche de Noël dates back to 1870, when the custom of burning a large log for good luck on the winter solstice started to go out of fashion. Pâtissiers picked up the tradition and started creating a cake in the shape. Now, pastry shops are filled with them all throughout December and January. They come in all different sizes, from cute miniature cakes (so you can try all the flavors) to sizes large enough for all those holiday gatherings.

This version is as simple as it is stunning! The filling is a rich milk chocolate French buttercream. (I've included a classic American buttercream option as well). Get the whole family involved and decorate the top with any holiday bits and bobs, such as festive sprinkles, miniature Christmas trees or little wrapped-up presents.

Baking spray, for pan
1 recipe Rolled Génoise Cake (page 105)

CHOCOLATE GANACHE
6 oz (170 g) bittersweet, semisweet or dark chocolate (60 to 70%), chopped
⅔ cup (160 ml) heavy cream

MILK CHOCOLATE FRENCH BUTTER-CREAM (SEE NOTE)
4 large egg yolks (~60 g)
½ cup (100 g) granulated sugar
¼ cup (60 ml) water
2 oz (60 g) milk chocolate
10 tbsp (1 stick + 2 tbsp [140 g]) unsalted butter, cubed, very soft

TO DECORATE
Powdered sugar

Spray a 10 x 15-inch (25 x 38-cm) jelly-roll pan with baking spray. Line with parchment going up the long sides to easily remove it from the pan. If it doesn't completely go up the short sides, that's ok. Spray the top of the parchment with baking spray as well (see picture page 104).

Preheat your oven to 350°F (175°C). Prepare and bake the rolled génoise cake batter.

As soon as you remove the cake from the oven, cover it with a damp cloth (it's okay if it touches the cake). This will keep the moisture in and help prevent any cracking. Allow to cool completely at room temperature in the pan.

MAKE THE CHOCOLATE GANACHE
Melt the chocolate either in the microwave or in a double boiler. Heat the cream just to a simmer and pour into the chocolate. Whisk to combine (see ganache tips, page 50). Keep at room temperature to cool and firm up, to easily spread on the outside of the bûche. If necessary, chill briefly in the refrigerator to speed this up, but keep a close eye on it so it does not get too firm to spread.

MAKE THE BUTTERCREAM

In the bowl of a stand mixer fitted with the whisk attachment, beat the egg yolks on medium speed for several minutes, until slightly lighter in color. In a small saucepan over medium-high heat, cook the granulated sugar and water to 244°F (118°C) and immediately remove from the heat. Let the bubbles calm down for a couple of seconds while giving the yolks one last quick whisk. Then, slowly pour the hot sugar syrup into the yolks while mixing on low speed. Avoid hitting the whisk with the syrup; instead, aim for the gap in between the side of the bowl and the whisk.

Once all the syrup has been added, increase the mixer speed to medium-high and whip until the bowl is cool to the touch, about 10 minutes. The egg yolks will initially look watery with the syrup addition, then lighten in color and thicken as the two are beaten together.

Meanwhile, melt the milk chocolate in a microwave or in a double-boiler, and set aside to cool as the buttercream finishes whipping.

Slowly add the very soft butter to the whipped egg yolks, 1 cube at a time, while whisking on medium speed. Then, whip in the melted milk chocolate.

ASSEMBLE THE CAKE

Remove the towel from the cooled génoise cake and transfer to a clean work surface, leaving the parchment paper on the bottom. Make sure your serving platter is nearby.

Spread the milk chocolate buttercream on top.

Roll from one of the short ends, using the parchment paper to help. It's a little awkward at first, but be patient, rolling a bit and then peeling away the parchment. Then, once you have the roll going, use the parchment to help move the cake. This allows for more even pressure when rolling. Don't press too hard, or the filling will ooze out the sides.

When you're just about at the end of the roll, transfer the cake and trailing parchment to the serving platter. Roll more to where the end of the cake is on the platter, and pull the parchment off.

TO DECORATE

Chill the cake for 30 minutes to firm up the buttercream. Trim the ends, if you'd like, with a serrated knife.

Using an offset metal spatula, spread the ganache on the outside, making long indentations to make it look like bark. Cover the ends as well, drawing a swirl with the end of a kebab skewer to mimic the cut-off end of the log.

Decorate with little presents, trees and/or reindeer. Then, dust with powdered sugar to top with a little snow and serve!

MAKE AHEAD

Lasts for 3 to 4 days in the fridge. Bring to room temperature before serving.

*See photo on page 102.

NOTE

To substitute a classic American buttercream filling, whip together 12 tablespoons (1½ sticks [170 g]) of soft unsalted butter with 2 cups (240 g) of powdered sugar. Then, mix in 2 ounces (60 g) of melted milk chocolate.

LIGHT-AS-A-FEATHER MOUSSE

The most popular mousse in France might just be our base recipe for this chapter, the mousse au chocolat, which dates back to 1755. Now, we aren't sure whether Charles Fazi, servant to Louis XVI, invented it, or the painter Toulouse-Lautrec, but the recipe is popular to this day for family Sunday lunches and commonly found on café dessert menus.

Mousse can be a stand-alone dessert as in The Frenchman's Chocolate Mousse (page 123), a main component in a fabulous dessert, such as the dainty strawberry mousse interior in the Charlotte aux Fraises (page 125) or a fancy dome in the Caramel Mousse Tartelettes (page 129), perfect for a fall dinner party.

Mousse can be made a variety of ways, but it all goes back to the texture: light, airy and luxurious! Whether you are blending a puree with whipped cream or melted chocolate with a light meringue, the key to mousse is making sure to keep as much air as possible in the mixture.

One last tip: Allow for plenty of time for the mousse to chill. This is when the flavor and airy texture develop. *Psst.* For that reason, mousse desserts are perfect to make ahead!

BASE RECIPE: THE FRENCHMAN'S CHOCOLATE MOUSSE

❧ SERVES 6 ❧

This recipe comes from François, my Frenchman, who knows how to make a handful of things from scratch: mayonnaise, salad dressing, cooked meats and, drumroll . . . chocolate mousse (which when combined can be a pretty darn good meal). When I lived in Paris, I took the train to visit him in Strasbourg. Each time I arrived, a big bowl of homemade chocolate mousse would be waiting for us in the fridge. Once we sat down to share it, two spoons would appear and a line of demarcation was drawn down the center. I always picked the bigger side.

He learned this recipe from a French friend of his and shared it with me. It is the classic way of making French chocolate mousse. The most important point to remember is to keep as much air as possible inside for that gorgeous light texture. To avoid deflating your mousse, carefully fold the ingredients together. Here is the technique: Dip the side of the spatula into the middle of the batter, scrape the bottom, then the side, bringing the batter from the bottom of the bowl up and over to the top. Turn the bowl slightly so you're working in a new spot, and repeat. As I fold, I recite in my head, "Into the middle, out to the sides."

6 large eggs

8 oz (225 g) bittersweet, dark or semisweet good-quality chocolate (60 to 70%), chopped (see Notes)

¾ cup (180 ml) heavy cream

Big pinch of salt

¼ cup (50 g) granulated sugar

Your choice of garnish: fresh berries, whipped cream, a sprinkle of unsweetened cocoa powder, cocoa nibs, shredded coconut . . . there are so many options!

Separate the egg yolks from the egg whites while they are cold, being careful not to get any yolk in the whites.

The easiest way to do this is by carefully cracking all the eggs into a bowl (I crack them into my stand mixer bowl, as we'll be whipping up the whites). Open up the eggs close to the bottom of the bowl so the yolks don't have a long way to fall. Alternatively, you can crack them individually in a small bowl, for extra security. Then, use a clean hand to scoop out the yolks and place them in a separate bowl. Open your fingers slightly to let the whites go through. Use an eggshell half to scoop out any yolk or tiny pieces of shell.

(CONTINUED)

MAKE THE GANACHE BASE

Melt the chocolate either carefully in the microwave or in a double boiler.

In a small saucepan, heat the cream until simmering (watch closely!), then pour, all in one go, over the chocolate. Whisk at the center of the mixture. Once it starts to thicken, whisk more energetically to bring the two ingredients together to form a thick ganache.

Whisk the egg yolks into the ganache and add the salt.

MAKE THE FRENCH MERINGUE

Whip the egg whites on medium speed, using the whisk attachment, until they resemble foam. When no liquid egg white is visible, increase the speed to medium-high. Gradually add the sugar, and whip until medium peaks form. See peak illustration on page 171.

FOLD EVERYTHING TOGETHER

Fold the whites into the ganache in thirds. For the first third, whisk in well to loosen up the texture. This will make it easier to incorporate the rest of the whites.

For the next third, switch to a spatula and carefully fold until just a couple of streaks remain. Then, fold in the remaining whites. See recipe description for helpful tips for folding. The goal here is to keep as much air in the mousse as you can! If a few clumps of egg whites remain here and there, it's best to leave them so the mousse doesn't deflate too much. For any clumps that are on top, run a spatula over them so they disappear and mix into the batter. The batter will seem a little runny, but will have body. The mousse firms up and the texture and flavor develop the longer it chills.

Transfer the mousse into the container in which it will be served: either small individual glasses or a large bowl that everyone can dig into family style. For the large bowl, cover with plastic wrap. For the small containers, if you'll be serving them in 3 to 4 hours, it's easiest to leave them unwrapped. If you plan to leave the containers overnight, though, it's best to cover them so the mousse doesn't dry out.

Small containers should chill for at least 3 hours before serving; even longer is better. A large serving bowl needs to chill overnight.

Bring to room temperature before eating for the most pronounced flavor. Decorate with your choice of garnish.

MAKE AHEAD

This is the perfect make-ahead dessert! Prepare the day before, for best results. Lasts for 3 days.

NOTES

Because mousse has very few ingredients, this is the time to spend a little more on eggs and pick up a higher-end chocolate. For chocolate brand suggestions and tips on forming a ganache (the base of this recipe), see page 50. Make sure to stick with bittersweet, dark or semisweet chocolate (60 to 70%), as called for in this recipe. If the type of chocolate is changed, the amount of cream will not be correct to make the consistency of ganache needed.

The longer it chills, the more complex the taste will be.

CHARLOTTE AUX FRAISES

❧ SERVES 10 TO 12 ❧

A ring of elegant ladyfingers surrounds a deliciously light strawberry mousse filling. This recipe is perfect for an afternoon of baking fun. The ladyfingers, mousse and Chantilly cream should be made the day of serving. The ladyfingers can wait on the counter for a couple of hours once they've baked, but you really want to assemble the whole dessert at one time. Remember to allow at least four hours for the mousse to firm up in the fridge before serving.

LADYFINGERS
5 large eggs

¾ cup (150 g) granulated sugar, divided

1 cup (125 g) all-purpose flour

Powdered sugar, for dusting

STRAWBERRY MOUSSE
3 cups (450 g) whole fresh or frozen and thawed strawberries

1½ tbsp (11 g) powdered gelatin (such as Knox brand) + ½ cup (120 ml) water, or 4½ gelatin sheets (see Notes)

¾ cup (150 g) granulated sugar

3 cups (720 ml) heavy cream, cold

TO ASSEMBLE
Baking spray

1 cup (150 g) fresh strawberries, sliced

CHANTILLY WHIPPED CREAM
1 cup (240 ml) heavy cream, cold

3 tbsp (24 g) powdered sugar

1 tsp vanilla extract, or ½ tsp vanilla paste

½ cup (75 g) fresh whole strawberries (pick the prettiest ones), for garnish

PREPARE THE PANS
Preheat your oven to 350°F (175°C).

Cut sheets of parchment paper to line two baking sheets. On the edge of one sheet, trace the outside of a 9-inch (23-cm) springform pan ring with a pencil. Leave room on the same baking sheet for another circle that will be piped freehand slightly smaller than the first. Flip the sheet over.

On the other piece of parchment, draw two rows to help pipe the ladyfingers. The rows will be connected once baked to form a ring around the cake. The height of the rows should be the height of the ring you're using (about 2½ inches [6 cm]). The combined length of the two rows should be long enough to encircle the inside of the springform ring (about 28 inches [71 cm]).

MAKE THE LADYFINGER BATTER
Carefully separate the eggs, placing the whites in the bowl of a stand mixer fitted with the whisk attachment, and the yolks in a small bowl. It's easiest to do this when they are cold. Make sure there is no yolk in the whites and that your mixer bowl is extra clean.

(CONTINUED)

Pour about half of the granulated sugar into the yolks and whisk well to combine. Set aside.

Start whisking the egg whites on medium speed until they resemble foam (you won't see any liquid egg white on the bottom of the bowl). Then, increase the speed to medium-high and very slowly add the remaining granulated sugar, about a tablespoon (15 g) at a time, waiting 15 seconds or so between each addition to allow the sugar to incorporate.

Keep whipping until all the sugar has been added, then check the peak. If it's not at stiff peak, whip a bit longer at a higher speed. This can take a total of 10 to 15 minutes to do! When you lift up the beater, the point should stand straight up.

Give the yolks a quick whisk and then drizzle over the whipped whites. Fold gently to combine. Fold in the flour in two additions, sifting the flour either into a bowl before adding, or sifting directly over the batter.

PIPE AND BAKE THE LADYFINGERS
Transfer to a piping bag fitted with a large round tip (10 to 12 mm; see chart, page 12).

Dab batter in the corners of the baking sheets and press the parchment paper on top to "glue" them in place. Pipe to fill in the inside of the traced circle, starting in the center and swirling out to the sides. The batter will be light and airy with bubbles.

Pipe ladyfingers in between the sets of lines you traced. The long edges should be touching. You can pipe them either straight or at an angle, your choice! Press with steady pressure to form a line. To stop, release the pressure and angle back over what you just piped and lift up (see picture).

With the remaining batter, working freehand, pipe a smaller circle next to the 9-inch (23-cm) circle on the first baking sheet. The small circle will be hidden inside and doesn't have to be perfectly round.

Liberally dust the ladyfingers and circles with powdered sugar. This forms a nice light crunch on the outside, and a beautiful finish.

Immediately bake for 15 minutes, switching the pans halfway through, until lightly golden brown. The circles might need a minute or two longer than the ladyfingers. It's normal for the ladyfingers to crack.

Remove from the oven and let cool completely on the baking sheets.

START THE STRAWBERRY MOUSSE
Hull the strawberries, cut in half and puree in a blender until smooth. You should have about 1½ cups (360 ml) of puree.

If using powdered gelatin, place it in a bowl and cover with ½ cup (120 ml) of cold water. Stir to coat and let sit about 5 minutes. For sheet gelatin, cover with cold water and let rest for about 5 minutes or until soft. Gently wring out the water, and place in a small bowl nearby.

(CONTINUED)

In a small saucepan, combine the strawberry puree with the granulated sugar and heat over medium-low heat until steaming. Turn off the heat and add the rehydrated gelatin. Stir until melted. Remove from the heat and let cool to room temperature, 30 to 45 minutes. While this cools, start assembling the charlotte.

ASSEMBLE THE CHARLOTTE

This is one of my favorite party tricks: To remove the parchment from the sticky ladyfingers and circles, gently turn over the cakes, with the paper still attached, onto a clean surface or fresh piece of parchment paper. Place a baking sheet on top to weigh down the cakes and to provide an edge to peel the paper against. Pull the paper up and back over the baking sheet. The used paper will peel off, leaving the cakes and ladyfingers cleanly removed.

Place the springform pan ring on your serving platter to support the charlotte while it's being assembled.

Line the inside of the ring with large strips of parchment reaching at least 2 inches (5 cm) higher than the rim. Lightly spray the inside with baking spray to help stick the parchment sheets to the sides. Don't spend a lot of time on this because as soon as the bottom layer of cake is put inside, it will press the paper in place.

Fit the 9-inch (23-cm) circle top down into the bottom of the ring, trimming if necessary with kitchen shears.

Line the inside of the ring with the ladyfingers, flush against the parchment paper. The two rows should fit together snuggly. If there are too many ladyfingers, trim with kitchen shears. I usually will leave what looks like one ladyfinger too much, as when you squish it in, it's a perfect fit.

FINISH THE MOUSSE

In the bowl of a stand mixer fitted with the whisk attachment, whip 3 cups (720 ml) of cold heavy cream to firm peak. Fold or delicately whisk in the cooled strawberry puree until smooth.

Pour half of the mousse onto the cake bottom. For a fresh burst of flavor, sprinkle the cup (150 g) of sliced strawberries on top. Put the smaller circle of cake inside and pour in the remaining strawberry mousse.

Chill for at least 4 hours for the mousse to set.

MAKE THE CHANTILLY WHIPPED CREAM

In the bowl of a stand mixer fitted with the whisk attachment, whip the heavy cream, powdered sugar and vanilla to medium-firm peak. It should be firm enough to hold its shape when piped. Pile it on top of the charlotte in billowy clouds swooped with the back of a spoon or in elegant piped swirls. Garnish with the ½ cup (75 g) of whole strawberries, styling as you'd like.

MAKE AHEAD

The cake can be prepared 1 to 2 days in advance, but is best the day it's made.

NOTES

If using sheet gelatin, sometimes the strengths are different. Check your package and follow the directions to gel 4 cups (1 L) of liquid.

If you want lots of dramatic height on top, increase the heavy cream for the Chantilly Whipped Cream by ½ cup (120 ml).

CARAMEL MOUSSE TARTELETTES WITH POACHED PEARS IN GINGER

Creamy caramel mousse is paired with refreshing ginger-poached pears on top of a crisp tart shell and finished off with candied pecans—a couple of easy components come together to make something incredible. These exquisite tarts are perfect to serve for a dinner party.

The key to this dessert is to assign parts of the recipe to do on certain days before the final assembly. I would suggest that you see the make ahead section, because there are so many ways to plot out making this dessert.

TART CRUST

½ recipe Pâte Sucrée (page 17)

¼ cup (1.5 oz [40 g]) chopped white baking chocolate, melted

GINGER-POACHED PEARS

3 cups (720 ml) water

1 cup (200 g) granulated sugar

1 (3″ [7.5-cm]) knob fresh ginger, peeled and chopped into large pieces

3 firm Bosc or Bartlett pears

CARAMEL MOUSSE DOMES

½ cup (120 ml) heavy cream

⅓ cup (80 ml) water

½ cup (100 g) granulated sugar

1 sheet gelatin, or 1 tsp powdered gelatin mixed with 2 tbsp (30 ml) water

1½ cups (360 ml) heavy cream, cold

CARAMELIZED PECANS (OPTIONAL)

⅓ cup (65 g) granulated sugar

½ cup (60 g) raw pecan halves

MAKE THE TART CRUSTS

Prepare the dough and chill until ready to assemble (up to 3 days in the fridge or 1 month in the freezer).

Line six individual tart pans (see Notes) and chill the shells in the freezer for 10 minutes before baking. Bake for about 15 minutes in a 325°F (165°C) oven, or until golden brown.

The tart crusts can be blind baked and cooked ahead and kept in an airtight container at room temperature for 3 days. Or bake them on the day you plan to serve them, for optimal crispiness.

The inside will be brushed with melted white chocolate when assembling the tarts.

(CONTINUED)

CARAMEL MOUSSE TARTELETTES WITH POACHED PEARS IN GINGER
❧ (CONTINUED) ☙

PREPARE THE GINGER-POACHED PEARS

In a medium-sized saucepan, bring the water, sugar and ginger to a boil.

Meanwhile, peel, quarter and core the pears. It's easier to core the pears after quartering them.

Reduce the heat of the poaching liquid to a simmer. Add the pears and simmer until soft, 30 to 45 minutes. How long you cook the pears entirely depends on how firm they are. To check that they are done, pierce the quarters with a knife. If the knife goes in with no resistance, they're cooked!

Turn off the heat and allow them to cool in the syrup (this will take several hours). Once cool, transfer to an airtight container and submerge the pears in the poaching liquid. Chill in the fridge until you're ready to use them (up to 3 days).

MAKE THE CARAMEL MOUSSE DOMES

In a small saucepan or in the microwave, heat the heavy cream just until it simmers. Then, remove from the heat.

Pour the water into a small saucepan with a light-colored interior (so you can see the caramel change color). Add the sugar in the middle of the pan. There's no need to stir; it will dissolve and spread as it's heated.

Place over medium-high heat and watch (not stirring) until the color starts to change. If needed, you can gently swirl the pan at this point to redistribute the heat.

When the caramel is a nice amber brown, remove from the heat and whisk in the warm cream, little by little, carefully avoiding the steam. It will bubble and gurgle like a cauldron.

Place a thermometer in the caramel to monitor the temperature. Let cool at room temperature for 10 to 15 minutes. When its temperature reaches 120°F (50°C), prepare the gelatin.

If using a gelatin sheet: Submerge in cold water until soft, about 5 minutes. Wring out the water and add to the caramel, mixing to combine.

If using powdered gelatin: Mix with the water, let sit for 5 minutes to rehydrate, then mix with the caramel. The caramel should have cooled to about 110°F (40°C) when the gelatin is added.

Continue to cool at room temperature for an additional 20 minutes or until neutral (not hot, not cold) to the touch. The temperature should be around 80°F (27°C).

In the bowl of a stand mixer fitted with the whisk attachment or in a large bowl, using an electric hand mixer, whip the cream to medium-firm peaks and then carefully fold in the caramel. Transfer to a piping bag with no tip and cut off the end to make a big round opening about ½ inch (1.3 cm) or so in diameter. You can always cut a larger opening if you find you're having to apply a lot of pressure for the mousse to come out.

(CONTINUED)

CARAMEL MOUSSE TARTELETTES WITH POACHED PEARS IN GINGER
❧ (CONTINUED) ❧

Place a 6-well silicone demisphere mold (see Notes) on a baking sheet and pipe the mousse inside to fill completely.

> ### NOTE
> To stop piping, stop applying pressure and then angle the bag completely horizontal to your surface and lift up.

Even off the tops, using an offset metal spatula.

Freeze overnight or up to 2 weeks.

MAKE THE CARAMELIZED PECANS
For the perfect garnish, toasted pecan halves are stirred in caramel for a nutty sweet crunch that is fantastic with this dessert. For more instructions on caramel, see page 159. If you're short on time, use toasted and chopped pecans instead.

Toast the pecans for 5 minutes at 350°F (175°C). Set aside to cool.

Line a baking sheet with parchment or a silicone baking mat. It's important to do this before starting the recipe, as once the nuts are stirred in the caramel, you need to turn them out immediately onto the baking sheet.

Place the sugar in a small skillet or saucepan with a light-colored interior so you can see the color change. Turn the heat to medium-high and wait, not stirring, until the sugar begins to melt and change color. At this point, using a heatproof spoon, stir briefly to redistribute the heat. It will look like icebergs. Stir briefly every once in a while until 75 percent of the sugar is melted. Then, stir to get rid of any clumps. Watch the heat and reduce it if the sugar seems to be browning too quickly. The caramel is done when it is a medium to dark amber and completely smooth.

Turn off the heat and add the toasted pecans and stir to coat. Distribute the pecan halves in a single layer on the lined baking sheet. I do this by dropping a couple of pecans from the pan at a time with a heatproof spoon, spreading them out a bit so the nuts aren't in one big clump.

Let cool completely and then finely chop.

Store in an airtight container in a cool, dry place (not the refrigerator as the humidity will soften them).

TO ASSEMBLE
Bake the tart shells, if you haven't already. Remove from the oven, let cool and brush the inside with melted white chocolate.

Chop the poached pears into small pieces. If it looks as if there's a lot of juice, drain in a sieve.

Fill the tart shells with the poached pears, pressing down to create a nice flat top.

Remove the mousse domes from the freezer and unmold, placing them on top of the pears (see picture 1 on next page).

Thaw for about 3 to 4 hours in the fridge before serving.

TO DECORATE
Decorate the sides and top with the finely chopped pecans (either simply toasted or caramelized). To arrange around the sides, pick up the tart in your less dominant hand. In your other hand, scoop up a bunch of chopped pecans and hold them in a cupped shape. Then, press up against the sides (see picture 2 on next page). Sprinkle a few nuts on the top of the dome (see picture 3 on next page).

STORAGE

The tarts are best eaten the day they are assembled. They will be good the following day as well; however, in that case, wait to decorate until serving.

MAKE AHEAD

Tart crust: 3 days ahead, stored in the fridge, or 1 month in advance, stored in the freezer.

Poached pears: 3 days ahead, stored in the fridge.

Caramelized nuts: 1 week in advance, stored at room temperature in an airtight container.

Caramel mousse domes: 2 weeks in advance, stored in the freezer.

NOTES

You can use conventional individual tart pans with the ruffled edge (4 inch [10 cm]), or small tart rings (3 inch [7.5 cm]) for a smooth edge. Both result in a gorgeous creation. When using the ruffled-edge tart pans, there will be some space in between the mousse dome and the edge of the crust. Fill in this gap with either toasted and finely chopped pecans or candied pecan pieces.

You will need a silicone demisphere mold for this recipe with 6 wells (2½ to 3 inches [6 to 7.5 cm] in diameter).

ROLLED RASPBERRY MOUSSE CAKE

❧ SERVES 6 ❧

Rolled cakes are often seen in France only around the holidays, with the traditional Bûche de Noël (page 118), but they are delicious any time of the year. Why not enjoy a raspberry rolled sponge cake for a summer *pique-nique*? It's easy to make and the perfect project for the whole family.

A raspberry mousse fills this fabulous rolled génoise cake. It comes together in a flash with just two ingredients: heavy cream and jam. Simply whip up the cream and then add the jam for a beautiful thick mousse to spread inside. Add even more flavor with fresh raspberries and more jam to this easy slice-and-eat cake!

Baking spray, for pan
1 recipe Rolled Génoise Cake (page 105)

SIMPLE RASPBERRY MOUSSE
1 cup (240 ml) heavy cream, cold
⅓ cup (110 g) raspberry jam (see Note)

TO ASSEMBLE
About ¼ cup (80 g) raspberry jam
1 cup (4 oz [125 g]) fresh raspberries
Powdered sugar, for dusting

Spray a 10 x 15-inch (25 x 38-cm) jelly-roll pan with baking spray. Line with parchment paper (it should go up the long sides, but if it doesn't entirely cover the shorter ends, that's totally fine; just crease the paper into the corners). Spray the top of the parchment with baking spray as well.

Prepare and bake the rolled génoise cake batter. Then, remove from the oven, cover with a damp tea towel and let cool in the pan.

MAKE THE SIMPLE RASPBERRY MOUSSE
In the bowl of a stand mixer fitted with the whisk attachment, whip the cold heavy cream at medium-high speed to medium peak and then add the raspberry jam. If the jam seems very thick (which will make it hard to incorporate), stir in a little water to thin it slightly before adding it to the whipped cream.

Continue beating the mixture to medium-firm peak to where it will hold its shape, scraping the bowl as needed. If the jam is not incorporating well, fold it in with a spatula.

ASSEMBLE THE CAKE
Remove the towel from the cooled génoise cake and transfer to a clean work surface, leaving the parchment paper attached to the cake. Make sure your serving platter is nearby.

Dot the top of the cake with the raspberry jam. Spread to cover the surface in a thin layer, using an offset metal spatula. This will help keep the cake nice and moist and add more *framboise* (raspberry) flavor!

Spread the raspberry mousse to cover the top, allowing for a 1-inch (2.5-cm) margin on the short ends.

Distribute the fresh raspberries on top, reserving a few for decorating, if you'd like! Press the raspberries into the mousse.

Roll from one of the short ends, using the parchment paper to help. It's a little awkward at first, but be patient, rolling a bit and then peeling away the parchment. Then, once you have the roll going, use the parchment to move the cake. This allows for more even pressure when rolling. Don't press too hard, or the mousse will come out the ends.

When you're just about at the end of the roll, transfer the cake and trailing parchment to your serving platter. This makes it much easier to move. Then, finish rolling the cake and pull the parchment completely off.

Cover with plastic wrap and chill for at least 30 minutes, or until ready to serve.

Before serving, cut off the ends with a serrated knife for a clean line. Waiting to do this until the cake has chilled and the filling has set will make this much easier!

Dust the top with powdered sugar and decorate with the reserved fresh raspberries (if using).

MAKE AHEAD

This cake can be made 1 day in advance. Keep chilled and covered with plastic wrap so it does not dry out.

NOTE

Use store-bought or homemade jam. I like the brand Bonne Maman®. The jam shouldn't be really runny, but it also shouldn't be super thick. You're looking for a good spreadable jam.

PÂTE FEUILLETÉE:
SUPER-SIMPLE PUFF PASTRY

In French, puff pastry is called pâte feuilletée, "layered dough." These legendary tiers create a buttery, flaky dough that is used for so many fabulous desserts. In a Tarte Tatin (page 147), a filling of caramelized apples melds perfectly with the crisp buttery puff pastry. Classic Mille-Feuilles (page 144), iconic sheets of pastry, shatter into a million flaky pieces on first bite, mixing beautifully with a smooth pastry cream.

To make puff pastry the traditional way, a big block of butter is encased in dough, then rolled and folded to create the layers. The whole finicky process can take up to two days and try the patience of the most dedicated baker.

Unless I had a super-easy method, I'd suggest you simply buy the best brand of puff pastry you can find. But what if I said you could make it in less time than it takes to go to the store? The base recipe you'll find in this chapter is so foolproof that after making it once or twice, you'll be quite the master, whipping up your own puff pastry in less than thirty minutes! Of course, in a pinch you can use a really good all-butter storebought for any of these recipes to make them extra simple and in a flash.

Leftover puff pastry? Don't throw away your scraps; instead, make cinnamon-sugar twists! Stack the scraps on top of one another (this makes sure you don't undo all the fabulous layers you've made), roll them out and then cut into strips. Toss in cinnamon sugar and place on a baking sheet, twisting each strip. Bake in a preheated 375°F (190°C) oven for fifteen minutes, or until golden brown. Enjoy!

BASE RECIPE: SIMPLE PUFF PASTRY

MAKES 2 SHEETS PUFF PASTRY (320 G TOTAL)

Simple puff pastry splits into irresistible buttery layers—the same as in the classic method—but the preparation takes minutes rather than days. Instead of wrangling with a butter block, the butter in the dough is left in big, manageable pieces. The high ratio—equal amounts—of butter to flour, plus the folds, creates the layers. When the butter melts in the oven, it creates steam, separating the layers, making that buttery flakiness we all love. Reach for this base recipe for any sweet or savory recipes that call for puff pastry. It can be easily doubled and any remaining dough frozen for a later date.

Worried about the folds? Don't be! It's as easy as folding a letter to put into an envelope!

1 cup (125 g) all-purpose flour, plus more for dusting
9 tbsp (1 stick + 1 tbsp [125 g]) unsalted butter, cold, cut into tablespoon-sized (14-g) pieces
4 to 6 tbsp (60 to 90 ml) cold water

MAKE THE DOUGH

Place the flour in a medium-sized bowl, then add the cold butter pieces.

Using your hands, toss the butter in the flour to coat the pieces. Then, pick up each butter piece and press to flatten between your thumbs and index fingers so they are easier to incorporate. If the lumps of butter break in half, or there are some smaller pieces, too, that's okay! Just remember, we need big pieces to create the puff! This should only take a minute—tops.

NOTE
If you're having to press really hard, it's because your butter is super cold. Wait a minute for it to warm up slightly before proceeding.

Start adding the cold water, 1 tablespoon (15 ml) at a time. Drizzle it over the flour and toss to incorporate with your hands, limiting how much you touch it. At the fourth tablespoon (a total of 60 ml) of water, squeeze the dough together to see how it holds a ball. Then, add more cold water to bring everything together—the quantity you need depends on how many floury bits are left in the bowl. The overall amount of water you use depends on your flour and the humidity! For example, on a rainy day, there's more moisture in the air, so you might add less water than on a hot, sunny day.

Your dough shouldn't feel dry or wet. If it feels dry, is cracking or has flour dust on the surface, scrunch in a few more drops of water. If your dough feels wet or sticky, this could be because your butter has started to melt or too much water was added. If your dough still feels cold, add a little more flour, scrunching in 1 teaspoon at a time (no kneading is necessary and try to limit how much you touch the dough). It won't take much flour to correct this. If the dough is soft, wrap it in plastic wrap and chill the dough before continuing with the folds.

Move on to the folds if your dough is still cold, but if you have time, I'd recommend chilling it for 15 minutes or even overnight before proceeding. This relaxes the dough, making it easier to work with and helps ensure those fabulous layers.

(CONTINUED)

PREPARE TO FOLD THE DOUGH

To create the layers, we'll be doing one single fold and two double folds. Flour your work surface (a good sprinkling), the top of your dough and the rolling pin (see picture 1 on page 138).

Start by rolling the dough into a long rectangle, the short end closest to you (see picture 2 on page 138). There's no precise measurement to how long your rectangle should be. You just want it long enough to make the folds (about two hands long will do the trick).

The most common problem you might run into is having your dough stick to the surface or your rolling pin. To fix this, after every couple of rolls, pick up the dough and move it around, coating the bottom with flour, and sprinkle more on your surface as needed. If you see any butter showing through to where the surface is tacky to the touch, or starts to stick to the rolling pin, tap some flour on top to provide a protective barrier.

WHAT TO LOOK FOR

The dough will be shaggy at first and then get smoother the more folds you do. You'll see big butter streaks in the first fold, then these will start to become less apparent as you go through the process. Your rectangles never have to be perfect! You want the dough to be cold, but not so cold that you're fighting to roll it out. You also never want it to be warm. Take your time and chill often for best results, particularly if your kitchen is warm.

SINGLE FOLD

For the first fold, treat the rectangle of dough as you would a letter to put into an envelope. Fold the bottom third up (see picture 3 on page 138), and brush off any excess flour on top. Then, fold the top third down (see picture 4 on page 138), covering the first third and forming a nice little rectangular packet (see picture 5 on page 138). If you have time, wrap in plastic wrap and chill for 15 minutes or longer in the fridge.

Turn the dough so the short end is facing you and roll it out again, just like before, into a long rectangle (see pictures 6 to 7 on page 138).

> ### TIP
> Make indentations in the dough packet by pressing the rolling pin on top before rolling it out (see picture 6 on page 138). This staples those layers together, helping the dough to roll out more evenly, and makes you look like a pro!

DOUBLE FOLD (2X)

Fold the short ends in to meet in the middle of the rectangle (see pictures 8 to 9 on next page). Brush off any excess flour, then fold the dough over on top of itself into another rectangle (see pictures 10 to 11 on next page). Chill the dough for at least 15 minutes for best results.

Turn the dough so you have the short side of the rectangle facing you. Roll out the dough into another long rectangle (see picture 12 on next page). Do one or two rolls widthwise to make it a bit wider (about the width of your palm).

Repeat the double fold once again (see pictures 8 to 12 on next page) to make the grand total of one single fold and two double folds (see picture 13 on next page to see the completed layers). Then, wrap the dough in plastic wrap and chill.

MAKE AHEAD

The dough can be made ahead and stored for 2 days in the fridge. You can freeze it for 1 month, well wrapped in plastic wrap and placed in a freezer bag. Thaw overnight in the refrigerator.

FYI: The dough might turn a very slight gray color in the fridge. It hasn't gone bad; this is due to oxidation. It won't affect the taste of the dough, and once baked, you won't be able to see it.

PALMIERS

⚜ MAKES 20 SMALL COOKIES ⚜

These little puff pastry treats, also called "elephant ears," are caramelized perfection. All you need to make palmiers is sugar and puff pastry! They're a buttery sweet treat made light and crunchy from the puff pastry. Roll them out in sugar, curl in the dough just so and then slice and bake! The sugar caramelizes in the oven like magic.

About ½ cup (100 g) granulated sugar, divided
1 recipe Simple Puff Pastry (page 139)
Baking spray, for pan (optional)

Cover a clean surface with a big handful of granulated sugar. Place the prepared puff pastry dough on top, then sprinkle some sugar on the dough as well. Roll out the dough into a large thin rectangle, about 9 x 13 inches (23 x 33 cm). Add more sugar as needed just as you would flour, to prevent the dough from sticking to your surface.

Roll the dough tightly from both of the long ends toward the center, rolling until they meet.

Wrap in plastic wrap and freeze for 10 to 15 minutes, or until cold and firm enough to cut like slice-and-bake cookies. Don't freeze too long, or the sugar will start to dissolve.

While the dough is chilling, preheat your oven to 425°F (220°C). Line a baking sheet with parchment or lightly spray it with baking spray. A silicone baking mat won't work here, as the nonstick surface will cause the palmiers to unroll.

Remove the dough from the freezer and use a serrated knife to cut ⅜-inch (1-cm)-thick pieces.

Coat the cut sides with sugar, then place on the prepared baking sheet.

Bake for 8 to 10 minutes, or until the bottom of the cookies is caramelized and the top edges are starting to brown. Don't worry if some butter leaks out of the dough. Remove from the oven and use a spatula to carefully flip the palmiers. Bake for another 3 to 5 minutes, or until golden brown. Watch closely as the timing varies by oven.

STORAGE

Keep in an airtight container at room temperature for up to 3 days.

MAKE AHEAD

Prepare the puff pastry in advance. Once the dough has been rolled in sugar, it cannot be frozen for longer than 15 to 20 minutes, or the sugar will start to dissolve.

VARIATIONS

Jam: After the puff pastry has been rolled into a big rectangle, brush or spread ¼ cup (60 g) of jam on top. Then, proceed with the instructions, skipping dipping the cut palmiers in sugar.

Flavored sugars: Use vanilla sugar or sugar rubbed with a tablespoon (6 g) of citrus zest (lemon, orange, lime, grapefruit . . .).

Spices: Mix a teaspoon of your favorite spice, or a blend of spices, into the sugar before using it in the recipe. Ideas include ground cinnamon or cardamom, or a mixture of ground ginger, cinnamon and cloves.

CLASSIC MILLE-FEUILLES

❦ MAKES 4 INDIVIDUAL CAKES ❧

Mille feuilles means "1,000 layers," referring to the sheets of puff pastry that make up this delicious dessert. Many top pastry shops and restaurants make mille-feuilles to order, for the utmost amount of crispiness. Pass your fork through the layers and they break into a million pieces, mixing with the luxurious pastry cream piped inside. The two textures contrast perfectly for quite a special treat! As a fun decorative flourish, I've added a recipe for Chantilly cream. Part of the cream will be folded with the pastry cream; the rest can be used to pipe in between the layers or on top! This is a bit different from a traditional mille-feuille, but I love how light it is in contrast to the often overly sweet coating of melted fondant that you can normally find on top.

1 recipe Vanilla Pastry Cream (page 35), or your flavor of choice

1 recipe Simple Puff Pastry (page 139) (see Notes)

All-purpose flour, for dusting

Fresh fruit (berries, slices of peach, figs, etc.) (optional)

Powdered sugar, for dusting

CHANTILLY CREAM

1 cup (240 ml) heavy cream, cold

¼ cup (30 g) powdered sugar

1 tsp vanilla extract

Make the vanilla pastry cream (page 35) and chill in the fridge while continuing with the rest of the recipe.

Line a baking sheet with parchment and find another baking sheet that will sit on top, level with the surface of the first one. (Ideally use two of the same kind of sheets that stack well. Alternatively, a big cooling rack flipped to be flush with the surface would work.)

Preheat your oven to 400°F (200°C).

Roll out the puff pastry ⅛ inch (3 mm) thick (about two pennies high), into a big, thin rectangle (about 10 x 13 inches [25 x 33 cm]).

As the dough gets thinner, there's more of a chance that it will stick, so remember to pick up and move your dough every couple of rolls and add more flour as necessary, underneath and on top. Don't worry too much about even, straight edges, as they will be trimmed after the puff pastry is baked.

To move the dough easily, fold it in half and half again. Place it on top of the prepared baking sheet and unfold. Prick the dough all over with a fork. Then, put another piece of parchment on top, completely covering the dough, and your second baking sheet on top of that to weigh it down. We want the crispiness but not the height.

Bake for 20 minutes.

Remove from the oven and take off the top baking sheet and parchment paper. Return to the oven and bake for another 5 to 10 minutes (or less!), or until the top is evenly golden brown. Keep an eye on it, as baking times will vary drastically by oven.

Remove from the oven and let cool completely.

(CONTINUED)

ASSEMBLE THE MILLE-FEUILLES

Trim your puff pastry so you have nice straight sides, cutting off as little as possible. Cut rectangles from your puff pastry using a serrated knife. You'll need three identical pieces for each pastry. The size and shape are completely up to you! You could even make one big pastry. For four individual pastries, the maximum size of each rectangle can be 2 x 4 inches (5 x 10 cm). It's easiest to make a cutout diagram from a piece of paper and then use this as a guide to cut out the shapes.

Remove the pastry cream from the fridge and whisk by hand just until smooth.

MAKE THE CHANTILLY CREAM

In the bowl of a stand mixer fitted with the whisk attachment or with a hand mixer, whip the heavy cream, powdered sugar and vanilla to medium-stiff peaks. Transfer about one-third of the Chantilly cream to the bowl of pastry cream. Whisk by hand to combine and lighten the pastry cream, making what is called a *diplomate* cream. Transfer to a piping bag fitted with a large round piping tip (10 mm; see chart, page 12) and set aside. Scoop the remaining Chantilly cream into another piping bag fitted with a star tip, for decoration.

Place one puff pastry rectangle on a serving platter. To fill, pipe big circles of the pastry cream mixture on top. You can alternate these with the Chantilly cream. I'll add pieces of fresh fruit to this as well. Place the next rectangle of puff pastry on top and repeat. Then, finish it off with the final piece of puff pastry.

TO FINISH

Sprinkle the top with powdered sugar and decorate with the Chantilly cream.

To be extra fancy, turn each assembled mille-feuille on its side and pipe the whipped cream on top. In the photo, I finished mine with a sprinkle of dried rose petals.

MAKE AHEAD

Follow the make ahead instructions for the pastry cream (page 35) and puff pastry (page 139). Bake the puff pastry and whip the cream on the day you want to assemble.

STORAGE

These are best eaten on the day they are made. They are delicious the following day, too, but the puff pastry will not be as crispy. Keep in the refrigerator.

NOTES

This recipe can easily be doubled.

To allow for more flexibility when rolling out the rectangle, consider increasing the puff pastry recipe by 50 percent (1½ cups [190 g] of flour and 13 tablespoons [1½ sticks + 1 tablespoon (190 g)] of butter). The water will increase to 6 to 8 tablespoons (90 to 120 ml). With the extra dough, you can focus on rolling to a certain thickness, but not have to worry about the exact shape. Once baked, trim as needed.

TARTE TATIN UPSIDE-DOWN CAKE

 SERVES 6

The tarte Tatin is assembled upside down and then flipped so the puff pastry is on the bottom and the apples sit like caramelized jewels on top. The flip might seem scary at first, but I've tweaked the recipe, suggesting that you assemble it in a cake or pie pan, instead of a bulky skillet. This makes it much easier to flip, so in the end, you feel like quite the accomplished pastry chef!

This classic French dessert was concocted in the 1880s at Hôtel Tatin run by sisters Stéphanie and Caroline Tatin. We aren't sure exactly how it came to be: whether an apple tart was dropped or if, in a moment of panic, a piece of puff pastry was thrown on top of apples that were caramelizing too quickly! What we do know is that the guests loved it and it soon spread to the rest of the country.

1 recipe Simple Puff Pastry (page 139)

4 to 5 firm apples (Braeburn, Jonagold, Pink Lady or Granny Smith)

Juice of ½ lemon

Unsalted butter, if using a cake or pie pan

½ cup (100 g) granulated sugar

5 tbsp (70 g) unsalted or salted butter, cubed

All-purpose flour, for dusting

Optional: ground cinnamon, dried culinary-grade or fresh lavender or chopped fresh rosemary or thyme

Start by making the simple puff pastry (page 139) so it has time to chill while you prepare the apples. Preheat your oven to 375°F (190°C).

Peel, quarter and core four of the apples. Crowd the apples, cut side up, on the bottom of the pan you'll be using to bake the tart to see how many you need (this will entirely depend on the size of the apple and the pan you use). I suggest an 8- to 9-inch (20- to 23-cm) round cake or pie pan, or you can use a traditional medium-sized skillet or, bien sûr, a Tatin dish. Because the apples will shrink a bit during cooking, throw in an extra apple quarter. Prepare and add the fifth apple, if needed.

Transfer the apple quarters to a bowl and toss with the lemon juice. This adds a bit of acidity to the recipe and helps keep them from oxidizing.

Generously butter the cake or pie pan (not necessary for the skillet or Tatin pan).

Place the sugar in a medium-sized skillet with a light-colored interior (so you can see the caramel change color). Melt undisturbed on medium heat, only stirring briefly with a heatproof spoon to help with even cooking. Once 75 percent of the sugar has melted, stir more to help melt and incorporate any clumps. The caramel is done when it is a medium to dark amber and completely smooth.

Turn off the heat and mix in the cubed butter. It will look separated; this is okay!

Next, using a pair of tongs, add the apples to the skillet, crowding them together. If you run out of space, you can do the following in two batches.

Turn on the heat to medium and cook for 5 minutes. The caramel will start to bubble up around the apples and come together. If it starts to smoke, the heat is too high and just needs to be lowered.

(CONTINUED)

Turn the apples over with the tongs to cook on the other side for another 2 to 3 minutes. They will look caramelized in color and smell divine.

Turn off the heat. Use tongs to transfer the apples to the prepared baking pan. Arrange them in a single layer, cut side up, nestled snuggly against one another. Then, pour the caramel over the mixture. If you are baking the Tatin in the skillet, simply arrange the apples into a single layer on the bottom of the pan.

Roll out the puff pastry to about ⅛ inch (3 mm) in thickness on a lightly floured surface, then measure a circle an inch or two (2.5 to 5 cm) bigger in diameter than the baking dish. The circle doesn't have to be perfect. I will hold the pan above the puff to get an idea of how big it needs to be and roughly cut it with a paring knife, kitchen scissors or a pizza cutter.

Dust the top of the apples with cinnamon, some lavender or rosemary or thyme (if using).

Drape the puff pastry over the apples, pressing gently and carefully around the edges to fill any gaps around the sides of the pan. Fold the excess dough back on itself to rest on the top in a ruffled, rustic pattern. Poke several holes with a knife through the dough to release steam as the tart bakes.

Bake for 45 to 50 minutes, or until golden brown all over.

After removing from the oven, let rest for at most 30 seconds for the bubbling to settle slightly (waiting any longer will cause the apples to stick to the pan when you flip).

Place a plate with sloped edges on top of the pan. Use a long, dry tea towel doubled up to flip the tart. This will give you much more control than oven mitts. It will get a little caramel on it, but just throw it in the wash! No biggie.

Flip the tart in one fell swoop! Be confident! Go for it! Move the plate off the towel, then use the towel to lift up the pan.

STORAGE

This is best the day it's made. Chill leftovers in the fridge and reheat in a preheated 350°F (175°C) oven for about 10 minutes.

MAKE AHEAD

Prepare the puff pastry in advance. Store for 2 days in the fridge or 1 month in the freezer.

NOTE
It is perfect served warm with a scoop of vanilla ice cream. To change up this dessert, consider using firm pears instead of apples.

GALETTE DES ROIS

 SERVES 6

After graduating from Le Cordon Bleu Paris, I started an internship at a little pâtisserie in January, a month ubiquitous in France for a special cake made for Epiphany: the *galette des Rois* (Kings' cake). There are two versions in France: the colorful brioche type made in the south of France, and this version, a delicious rich almond cream encased in flaky, buttery puff pastry. Before baking, the pâtissier always slips a *fève,* a lucky charm, into the galette. The French tradition is that the youngest in your party gets under a table and calls out the name of a person to receive a slice. This way, no one has an advantage of picking the slice that contains the fève, since the person that wins is the king or queen for the day!

2 recipes Simple Puff Pastry (page 139)

ALMOND CREAM
5 tbsp (70 g) unsalted butter, cubed, at room temperature

⅔ cup (80 g) powdered sugar

1 cup (95 g) ground almonds

2 tbsp (15 g) all-purpose flour

1 large egg

1½ tsp (8 ml) vanilla extract

¼ tsp almond extract

1 to 2 tbsp (15 to 30 ml) rum (optional)

All-purpose flour, for dusting

1 beaten egg, for the egg wash

Start by making the simple puff pastry (page 139).

PREPARE THE ALMOND CREAM
In the bowl of a stand mixer fitted with a paddle attachment, or in a medium bowl and using a whisk, mix together the butter and powdered sugar until smooth and lighter in color. The butter has to be nice and soft to do this.

Incorporate the ground almonds and flour.

Scrape down the bowl, mix again, and then add the egg, vanilla and almond extracts and rum (if using), beating until smooth. If using a mixer, you will need to scrape down the bowl several times for an even mix. Chill the almond cream in the fridge while you work on the puff pastry.

ASSEMBLE THE PASTRY
On a floured surface, roll out the puff pastry into a long rectangle, long enough to be able to cut out two 9-inch (23-cm) circles. Use a 9-inch (23-cm) round cake pan or salad plate to estimate. Don't cut out the circles, though; we are just measuring for length.

Cut the rectangle of dough in half crosswise and transfer one portion to a parchment-lined baking sheet. Use a smaller ring or soup bowl (about 6 inches [15 cm] in diameter) to lightly indent a circle to act as a guide for where to put the almond cream. Leave about a 1-inch (2.5-cm) margin between the edge of the smaller circle and the edges of the dough.

Spoon or pipe the almond cream inside to fill the indented circle. Place a fève (see Note) in the almond cream for a lucky person to find. Then, brush the exposed dough with water, either with a pastry brush or crumpled paper towel. Water works better than egg wash for sticking together dough.

(CONTINUED)

Turn the other square of puff pastry 90 degrees and place on top. The quarter turn will help the puff pastry keeps its circular shape. If you're not sure what the turn would be as things have moved around in the kitchen (it happens!), just make sure that the 2 cut edges from the original rectangle aren't on top of each other. Smooth the dough around the almond cream to prevent air bubbles and press gently to seal the 2 pieces together.

Place the 9-inch (23-cm) cake pan guide on top, making an indentation. Remove, and use a paring knife to cut along the line so you have a circle.

For a scalloped edge (as in the photo), use the dull side of a knife to push the sides in toward the center of the cake every inch or so.

In a small bowl, beat the egg with a fork to make an egg wash and brush on top, right up to the edge, using either a pastry brush or crumpled-up paper towel. Be careful not to get any on the sides, as this can prevent the puff pastry from rising. Reserve leftover egg wash.

Chill the unbaked cake for 15 minutes.

Remove from the refrigerator and brush the top again with egg wash. The layers of egg wash will intensify the golden hue while baking.

BAKE THE CAKE

Preheat your oven to 400°F (200°C).

Use a sharp paring knife to score the top in whatever design you'd like, being careful not to cut through to the almond cream. To release the steam as the galette bakes, make a small cut in the center, making sure to cut all the way through to the filling. Make two more cuts on the top (I line the holes up with the scores I've made, to "hide" them).

Bake for 40 to 45 minutes, or until deep golden brown.

Remove from the oven and serve warm.

MAKE AHEAD

This can be cooled completely and stored covered at room temperature for 2 to 3 days until ready to be served. To reheat, place in a 325°F (165°C) preheated oven for 10 to 15 minutes, or until hot to the touch.

Prepare the puff pastry 2 days in advance, then store in the refrigerator or freeze for up to 1 month (thaw overnight in the fridge).

The almond cream can be made 2 days in advance. Keep chilled.

You can also fill and assemble the galette des Rois and chill it overnight, unbaked and covered, or even freeze it! Do the egg wash right before you bake it.

NOTE
Add a fève (small porcelain figurine) that is made to be baked, or something else, such as an uncooked bean or almond, that will identify the winner as the king or queen for the night.

SAINT-HONORÉ

❧ SERVES 6 TO 8 ❧

This dessert was created in 1847 by Chiboust pâtisserie on rue Saint-Honoré in Paris. It also happens to be the name of the patron saint of bakers in France! It evolved from being a pastry cream–filled brioche to what it is today: an iconic French dessert that I love to describe as cream upon cream with a caramel crunch and flaky puff pastry. The base is puff pastry topped with a swirl of pâte à choux dough. Caramel-dipped, vanilla pastry cream–filled cream puffs are arranged around the edge. Then, the center is finished off with a layer of luscious pastry cream.

1 recipe Simple Puff Pastry (page 139)
1 recipe Vanilla Pastry Cream (page 35)
1 recipe Pâte à Choux (page 83)
All-purpose flour, for dusting
⅓ cup (80 ml) heavy cream, cold

CARAMEL
⅓ cup (80 ml) water
1 cup (200 g) granulated sugar

CHANTILLY WHIPPED CREAM
¾ cup (180 ml) heavy cream, cold
1 tsp vanilla extract or paste
2 tbsp (16 g) powdered sugar

Make the simple puff pastry (page 139) and vanilla pastry cream (page 35). Chill in the fridge while continuing with the rest of the recipe.

Next, make the pâte à choux (page 83). You'll need 8 to 10 cream puffs for the top of the Saint-Honoré. I like to have extras, though, so I can pick the best ones, so I recommend piping 15. Reserve about ½ cup (150 g) of the excess pâte à choux dough for a later step. The rest of the dough can be piped and frozen for later (see tips, page 84), made into Chouquettes (page 90) or mixed with a big handful of shredded cheese and baked to make gougères (baking time and temperature is the same as for chouquettes).

Preheat the oven to 375°F (190°C) and line a baking sheet with parchment or a silicone baking mat. Transfer the dough to a piping bag with a 10 to 12 mm piping tip (see piping tip chart, page 12).

Pipe 15 walnut-sized mounds (1 inch [2.5 cm] in diameter) on the prepared pan. Use a wet finger to pat down any tips, then bake for 25 to 30 minutes, or until a deep golden brown. Remember to not open the oven while they are baking.

While the choux are baking, roll out the puff pastry on a lightly floured surface to ⅛ inch (3 mm) thick. Cut out the shape you'd like to make your Saint-Honoré: a long rectangle, a square or a circle. Always cut the shape a little larger than you'd like it to be, as it will shrink a little while baking. A good rule of thumb is to use a 9- to 10-inch (23- to 25-cm) cake pan as a guide.

Transfer to a baking sheet lined with parchment paper or a silicone baking mat. Pipe an open swirl on top with the reserved pâte à choux dough, leaving a 1-inch (2.5-cm) margin around the perimeter. This will keep the puff pastry from puffing too much in the oven and add an even more interesting texture and taste to the base. The space in between the swirls of dough will be filled with pastry cream after it's baked.

When the choux puffs are done, pop the base in the oven and bake at 375°F (190°C) for 25 to 32 minutes (depending on the size), or until nicely browned all over. Remove from the oven and let cool.

(CONTINUED)

FILL THE CREAM PUFFS

Whisk the chilled pastry cream briefly by hand for a smoother texture. Whip up the ⅓ cup (80 ml) cold heavy cream to medium-firm peak in a mixer fitted with a whisk attachment and whisk it into the pastry cream for a lighter texture. (You can use this mixer bowl again later to whip up the Chantilly cream.) Transfer to a piping bag fitted with a small round tip (5 to 6 mm).

Pick the cream puffs you would like to use to decorate the top edge of your puff pastry base. Think about grabbing one to place in the middle, too. Poke a hole in the bottom with a chopstick or knife to make it easier to insert the piping tip.

Fill each cream puff with the lightened pastry cream (see picture 1). You'll know they're full when they feel heavy in your hand and a little cream comes out the end when you pull the piping tip out. This can be scraped away on the side of the bowl or with a clean finger.

Only fill the choux you'll be using for decoration to allow for leftover pastry cream to swirl on the inside of the cake.

PREPARE THE CARAMEL

The caramel is to dip the tops of the cream puffs into and to stick them to the base. Place the water in a small saucepan with a light-colored interior so you can see the color change. Then slowly pour the granulated sugar inside, aiming for the middle of the pan (don't stir). Cook on medium heat until it starts to change color (no stirring!). At this point you can gently swirl the pan if needed to redistribute the heat. Cook to a medium amber (it will continue to darken slightly after you turn off the heat).

Remove the caramel from the heat. Use a dry tea towel to prop the pan up at an angle so the caramel will pool to one side. This will give you access to a deeper amount, making it easier to dip the choux.

Wait for the bubbles to subside, then carefully dip the top of each filled cream puff into the caramel (see picture 2 on previous page). Allow the excess to drip off. Then, watch how the caramel falls; you can either scrape the last bit of run-off on the side of the pan or rotate the cream puff to incorporate it on the top. If you get any hot caramel on your hands, immediately wipe it off on your apron or a kitchen towel. Reheat the caramel over low heat, if necessary, or make a second batch.

Place the choux, caramel side up, on a sheet of parchment or a silicone baking mat to cool. They start to cool within a matter of seconds.

Use the remaining caramel to "glue" the cream puffs around the edge of the base of puff pastry. Carefully dip one side of the bottom into the caramel and then stick to the puff pastry. I start with the first choux I dipped, so the top is cool and hard. Traditionally, the choux are placed in a ring right beside one another around the edge of the base, but it looks nice with space between the choux, too. I like to reserve one for the top as well!

Pipe the remaining pastry cream on top of the base.

FINISH WITH THE CHANTILLY WHIPPED CREAM

In the bowl of a stand mixer fitted with the whisk attachment or in a large bowl, using an electric hand mixer, whip the heavy cream, vanilla and powdered sugar on medium-high speed until it reaches a medium-firm peak (essentially to where it will hold a shape when piped). If you accidentally overwhip, stir in un-whipped cream to fix it.

Transfer to a piping bag. Traditionally, a tip named after the cake is used (Saint-Honoré; see chart, page 12). It has a slit on the side and produces a gorgeous ruffle shape or, even more classic, a line of dashes. If you don't have this tip, you can try cutting a little off the bottom of a disposable pastry bag to make a round opening and then cut a slit on the side. Or simply use another kind of tip—this is your cake, after all! Pipe the whipped cream (with the slit facing up and your bag at an angle) on top of the pastry cream and in between the cream puffs. If you reserved a cream puff, this can be placed on top for a finishing touch.

Serve the day it's made.

MAKE AHEAD

There is a lot you can do to make this dessert easier by making the components in advance. Prepare the simple puff pastry up to 2 days before, chilling the dough until you're ready to work with it, or use store-bought puff pastry.

Make the pastry cream up to 3 to 5 days in advance. The pâte à choux, caramel, and Chantilly cream need to be made on the day the cake is assembled. *See photo on page 136.

NOTES

Change up this recipe by playing around with different flavors of pastry cream. The size and shape of the cake are up to you as well. Usually it comes as a large circle or rectangle, but these can be made individual-sized, too. The components remain exactly the same!

I included a large amount of caramel for dipping the choux for safety reasons (I'd rather a little sugar be wasted than you have burnt fingers!). To clean the pan, add a lot of water and let it simmer away on the stove until the caramel at the bottom of the pan has dissolved. Turn off the heat and then clean as normal!

CRISP OR GOOEY
CARAMEL

Caramel at its base is simply sugar, cooked until it changes color and starts smelling incredible! It can be turned into a thick and delicious sauce (page 159), a crisp golden coating on cream puffs for a Croquembouche (page 99), mixed in to flavor a chocolate ganache (page 49) and so much more! Funnily enough, there's not a whole lot to it. The hardest part is watching and waiting for the sugar to caramelize, and resisting the urge to stir!

Caramel has always been my absolute favorite thing to eat, but when I started baking, I found it so intimidating! The recipes were sprinkled with warnings and it looked so complicated. Now it has become one of my favorite things to teach—busting that myth that caramel is hard. My most important tip: Remember it's just sugar melting and cooking, and like a good steak, it needs time to simply sit and caramelize.

Instead of constantly warning you throughout the recipes, all you need to remember is that caramel is HOT. It's hot during the cooking process, and after. So, no fingers in the caramel trying to get a taste before it's cooled, no matter how delicious it looks (this goes for all caramel recipes). Wait for it to cool and then snag a bite; it will taste better then, too, promise. The other tip, when adding cream or butter to a caramel, is to be sure to use a saucepan with tall sides. It will bubble up to two to three times its size, so we want to make sure it stays inside. And last, but certainly not least, always use a heatproof spoon. Many a plastic spatula has met a slow demise when making caramel.
Oh, sweet caramel!

BASE RECIPE: MOLLY'S FAVORITE SALTED CARAMEL SAUCE

⤞ MAKES 1 CUP (240 ML) ⤝

I could eat this by the spoonful! It's the ultimate combination of buttery and salty. Pour it over ice cream, cakes, brownies, cream puffs and everything in between. Enjoy! Just like ganache, depending on how caramel is made and what is added, it will be crisp or chewy, liquid or firm! At its base, just sugar and maybe water, the finished caramel will harden when cooled, making it a fun tasty decoration. Add a bit of cream, butter or even a fruit puree, and suddenly it turns thick and chewy—yum!

You can make caramel using two different methods. The dry method involves just sugar, cooked in a dry pan with nothing else until it caramelizes. The wet method adds water to the sugar, boiling the two together until the water evaporates and the sugar turns into a thick syrup. Once it hits a certain temperature, the syrup starts to change color. There are situations when to use both—for the dry method, you have less risk of crystallization and it's often faster, but you have less control over the color. For the wet method, the process is less hands-on and you are able to regulate the color. The wet method is used for this recipe so we can carefully watch for a light-medium amber color.

The smoke point: When your caramel is the darkest it will be, tendrils of smoke will puff from the pan. This is when to remove the caramel from the heat, as past this, it will start to burn.

Crystallization: Sugar, scientifically speaking, is a crystal and it wants to remain as such. By cooking it, we are forcing it to change into a liquid. When the caramel changes from being liquid back to what resembles sugar, a clumpy and white powdery mass, it has crystallized. This happens most often when you stir. The best way to keep it from happening, sit back, relax, pour a cup of tea and let the sugar simply cook. If you notice crystals forming on the side of your pan, this is crystallization. The easiest way to fix this is to cover the pan with a lid. The steam will collect and then go down the sides, washing them away. You can also brush down the sides with water.

Sticky pan? Fill it full of hot water and wait for the caramel to dissolve. To speed up the process, simmer it on the stove. Add the spoon you used, too, to clean off any stuck-on bits.

(CONTINUED)

BASE RECIPE: MOLLY'S FAVORITE SALTED
❧ CARAMEL SAUCE (CONTINUED) ❧

½ cup (120 ml) heavy cream
⅓ cup (80 ml) water
1 cup (200 g) granulated sugar
4 tbsp (½ stick [55 g]) unsalted butter, cubed, at
room temperature
½ tsp fleur de sel (salt)

Heat the cream either in a microwave or in a small saucepan on the stove until just simmering. Remove from the heat, cover and set aside.

Pour the water into a small to medium-sized saucepan with high sides. Then, pour the sugar into the middle of the pan, avoiding the sides. Don't stir, even if the sugar is in a mound. It will dissolve into the water as it heats up.

Cook over medium heat, not stirring, until the mixture starts to boil across the entire surface. Cover the pan with a lid for 30 seconds to 1 minute, to wash the sides and prevent any crystals from forming.

Remove the lid and continue to cook. The bubbles will start to change as the water evaporates and it becomes a thick syrup (yet again, no stirring needed!). Gently swirl the pan when you see color, if necessary, to redistribute the heat.

Cook the caramel to a light-medium amber brown, turn off the heat and pour in the warm cream in two additions. After each addition, let it bubble up and then stir with a heatproof spoon to combine, avoiding the steam. Adding it in two additions will help keep the cauldronlike effects to a minimum. Stir in the butter and salt. If there are any hard pieces, turn the heat back on to low and stir to dissolve.

Let cool (don't sneak a taste until then) and transfer to an airtight container.

STORAGE

Store in an airtight container in the refrigerator for 2 weeks or freeze for 1 month. Thaw frozen caramel at room temperature or in the fridge. Warm in a microwave, or in a small saucepan over low heat.

NOTE
I almost always take my caramel to a deep amber color before adding the cream. Not in this case! The flavor is even better when the color of the caramel is at light-medium amber when the cream and butter are added.

CRÈME CARAMEL

⚞ SERVES 6 ⚟

Crème caramel is quite the elegant dessert! It's a beautiful little flan dotted with vanilla bean seeds, with a golden top that sits in a pool of caramel. Bring a little bit of France to your dinner party with this recipe. It is best made the day before, as it needs to chill overnight to develop the flavors, and is good for three days, making it the perfect bake-ahead treat. The only slightly difficult part is making the dry caramel at the beginning. Just read the directions carefully, and since it's a large quantity of sugar to caramelize, stir it in little by little.

CRÈME
1 vanilla bean, or 1 tbsp (15 ml) vanilla bean paste

2¼ cups (540 ml) whole milk

4 large eggs, at room temperature

⅓ cup (65 g) granulated sugar

CARAMEL
1 cup (200 g) granulated sugar

BEGIN THE CRÈME
Cut the vanilla bean in half and scrape out the seeds. Add the seeds and bean (or the vanilla bean paste) to a medium-sized saucepan along with the milk and bring to a simmer over medium heat. Whisk to disperse the vanilla bean seeds. Turn off the heat and cover the pan. Set aside to gently infuse while you prepare the rest of the recipe.

Preheat your oven to 350°F (175°C).

Place six individual (4- to 6-ounce [120- to 200-ml]) ramekins in a large casserole dish or roasting pan.

MAKE THE CARAMEL
As we are using a large quantity of sugar, we will melt it *petit à petit*, using the dry method, before pouring it into the ramekins. Pour in enough of the sugar to coat the bottom of the saucepan you are using. It should be at most ¼ inch (6 mm) thick. I use a medium-sized saucepan with a light interior to see the color change. A skillet would work as well, as we won't be adding any cream, which would cause it to bubble up to great heights.

Place the saucepan over medium heat and wait several minutes (not stirring) for the layer of sugar to melt. There's no walking away from this one. Wait by the stove, as the color can change quite quickly. When the sugar starts to turn very brown in an area, use a heatproof spoon to draw lines through the sugar once or twice gently to redistribute the sugar in the pan (it will look like icebergs [see picture below]). When 75 percent of the sugar has melted, stir to melt the larger pieces, then add some more sugar to the pan.

NOTE
If the caramel seems to be darkening too quickly, turn down the heat! If the sugar starts to clump up and feel thick, hang tight. Stop stirring and turn down the heat a little to just let it melt.

(CONTINUED)

CRÈME CARAMEL (CONTINUED)

Allow it to melt, then just as before, draw a heatproof spoon through the sugar to briefly move it around. Continue like this until all the sugar is in the pan. When just about all of the sugar has melted, stir to finish the caramel and to get rid of any lumps. Bring to a dark amber color.

Immediately pour and divide the hot caramel equally among the ramekins. Don't wait too long, or it will start to harden in the pan.

FINISH THE CRÈME

In a large liquid measuring cup, whisk together the eggs and sugar. This will make it easier to pour into the ramekins. Remove the vanilla bean pod from the milk. While whisking, drizzle into the eggs. Distribute the batter equally among the ramekins.

Carefully add enough boiling water to the casserole dish to come halfway up the sides of the ramekins. Avoid splashing it into the ramekins. Bake for 30 to 35 minutes, or until the crème caramel is set. Gently jiggle one with tongs, reaching into the oven, to see. It should be firm but wiggle slightly.

After you remove the ramekins from the oven, carefully transfer them from the hot water to a wire rack, using a pair of tongs. Let cool to room temperature. Then, cover and chill overnight.

NOTE

The easiest way to chill the ramekins is to place them in a large casserole pan or on a large platter and cover everything with plastic wrap.

Serve cold. Run a knife around the inside of each ramekin. Dip the bottom in hot water for several seconds, dry it and then flip onto a plate and gently shake to release. This will create a suction, so they usually won't just flop out.

If you have a kitchen torch, this is a great time to use it. Instead of dipping the ramekins in water, after you've run a knife around the inside edge, turn them upside down on the plate. Then, run the flame briefly across the bottom, shaking gently to release.

MAKE AHEAD

These will keep for 3 days in the fridge. Enjoy cold and unmold just before serving.

NOTE

If you don't have small ramekins, this recipe can be baked in an 8-inch (20-cm) round cake pan. Increase the baking time to 45 to 50 minutes.

SPICED CARAMEL APPLE CREAM PUFFS

What better way to celebrate fall than relaxing by the fireplace with a spiced caramel apple cream puff in one hand and hot apple cider in the other? My salted caramel sauce is stirred into the cooked apples, whipped into cream and even drizzled on top. A fantastic way to get full use out of this delicious base recipe.

1 recipe Cream Puffs (page 85)
1 recipe Molly's Favorite Salted Caramel Sauce (page 159), divided

SAUTÉED SPICED APPLES
3 large or 4 medium-small Gala apples, peeled, cored and chopped
3 tbsp (40 g) unsalted butter, cubed
2 tbsp (30 g) dark brown sugar
1 tsp ground cinnamon
½ tsp ground ginger

CARAMEL WHIPPED CREAM
1½ cups (360 ml) heavy cream, cold

Bake the cream puffs and allow to cool.

Make the caramel sauce. Watch the color of the sugar carefully, cooking it to only a light-medium amber. Allow to cool completely at room temperature.

MAKE THE SAUTÉED SPICED APPLES
In a large skillet, sauté the chopped apples in the butter, brown sugar, cinnamon and ginger for 5 to 10 minutes. The cooking time depends highly on the apple and could be longer (if needed, add a little water to the pan to keep the apples from sticking). When they can easily be pierced with a knife, they're cooked. Turn off the heat and stir in ¼ cup (60 ml) of the caramel sauce. Let cool completely.

MAKE THE CARAMEL WHIPPED CREAM
In the bowl of a stand mixer fitted with the whisk attachment, whip the cold heavy cream to medium-firm peak. Add ¼ cup (60 ml) of the caramel sauce (see Note about consistency) to the whipped cream. Then, continue to whip until combined. Scrape the bowl as necessary to help incorporate the caramel. Transfer to a piping bag fitted with a large star tip.

Cut the cream puffs in half and fill with the apples. Top with the caramel whipped cream and a drizzle of caramel sauce.

STORAGE
Serve immediately or chill for several hours or up to overnight. These are great the next day, too.

MAKE AHEAD
Make the pâte à choux for the cream puffs in advance following the make ahead tips on page 84. The apples can be made 3 days in advance and kept chilled.

NOTE
If the caramel sauce seems very thick, it won't incorporate well into the whipped cream, so instead of fighting with it, omit it from the whipped cream and add more to the cooked apples.

CHOCOLATE-CARAMEL-NUT TART

SERVES 10 TO 12

This pastry is a marriage of two very classic caramel tarts. Often you'll see a caramel tart made by pouring caramel over nuts in a tart crust. Another very traditional version has a thick layer of caramel topped with a chocolate glaze.

I melded these two tarts together and it is nothing short of spectacular! A chewy caramel coats the bottom of a sweet tart crust. On top of this, there is a swirl of chocolate caramel *crémeux* (a creamy ganache). To finish, lots of salty toasted nuts are sprinkled on.

This is a good make-ahead dessert, as it tastes even better the day after it's made!

½ recipe Pâte Sucrée (page 17), vanilla or chocolate

CHOCOLATE CARAMEL CRÉMEUX
6 oz (170 g) bittersweet chocolate, 60%, chopped

2 tbsp (28 g) unsalted butter, room temperature, cubed

1 cup (240 ml) heavy cream

⅔ cup (130 g) granulated sugar

CHEWY CARAMEL
⅓ cup (80 ml) heavy cream

⅓ cup (80 ml) water

1 cup (200 g) granulated sugar

2 tbsp (28 g) unsalted butter, cubed, room temperature

TO DECORATE
1 cup (150 g) salted and roasted nuts (cashews, peanuts, pistachios, almonds . . .)

Powdered sugar, for dusting

Make the pâte sucrée dough (page 17) first so it has 45 minutes to chill before you roll it out.

PREPARE THE CHOCOLATE CARAMEL CRÉMEUX
This will need 1½ to 2 hours to set in the fridge before using.

Place the chocolate in a medium-sized heatproof bowl and the butter nearby so it's ready to go.

Heat the cream to a simmer in a microwave or a small saucepan. Cover and set aside. This step will help prevent the caramel from seizing when we add it later.

Make a dry caramel by spreading the sugar on the bottom of a medium-sized saucepan. You want a relatively thin layer of sugar on the bottom (¼ inch [6 mm]). I use a pot that is 8 inches (20 cm) in diameter. Heat over medium heat to melt the sugar. Wait by the pot, as the color can change quite quickly. When the sugar starts to bubble and turn brown in areas, draw a heatproof spoon once or twice through the sugar to redistribute the heat in the pan. When 75 percent of the sugar has melted, stir to get rid of any lumps and bring to a deep amber color (see picture page 161).

Turn off the heat.

Adjust the heat as needed—turning it up if the sugar is melting too slowly and down if you start to see smoke or want a little more control. Color is hard to regulate with a dry caramel and it often smokes at the end. Luckily all we want here is a nice deep caramel. Take it off the heat as soon as everything is melted and start adding the cream to stop the cooking.

Carefully whisk in the warm cream in several additions, avoiding the steam. Then whisk in the butter. If the caramel separates from the cream, put it back on the stove on low heat, whisking until the caramel melts and everything comes together.

Pour the hot caramel over the chocolate and whisk to create a crémeux.

Cover with plastic wrap, touching the crémeux, and chill until cold but pliable, 1½ to 2 hours. Watch the texture carefully if you plan on piping it on top so it doesn't get too firm.

BAKE THE TART CRUST

Meanwhile, line a 9- to 9½-inch (23- to 24-cm) tart shell or 6 individual tart shells (4 inches [10 cm] in diameter) with the pâte sucrée, bake and let cool.

MAKE THE CHEWY CARAMEL

Heat the heavy cream to a simmer either in a microwave or in a small saucepan.

In a small to medium saucepan, add the water. Carefully pour the sugar in the middle of the pan (no need to stir). Turn the heat to medium and cook (not stirring), watching it bubble away, until it is a dark amber. This can take awhile, so stick around and maybe turn on some tunes. For the darkest caramel, look for when it reaches the smoke point (a thin wisp or puff of smoke will appear).

Immediately take off the heat and stir in the butter with a heatproof spoon or whisk. Then mix in the cream.

Pour to coat the bottom of the baked crust(s).

Cool at room temperature or in the fridge until the chocolate crémeux is ready to use.

ASSEMBLE THE TART

Once the crémeux is chilled but pliable, either spread it on top of the caramel or transfer it to a piping bag fitted with a large round tip (10 to 12 mm; see chart, page 12) and swirl it on top, starting in the middle and working your way out to the edge.

Cover the top with the nuts and a light dusting of powdered sugar! Keep cool in the fridge. Remove 30 minutes before serving to take off the chill.

MAKE AHEAD

This tart tastes best if prepared the day before, to allow the flavors to meld together. It will last for 3 days in the fridge. The crémeux can be made 2 days before assembling, but might need to be left at room temperature to soften before spreading or piping on top. The tart shell(s) can be baked several days in advance and kept in an airtight container at room temperature; otherwise, make the dough ahead. *See photo on page 156.

MERINGUE SUGAR CLOUDS

Meringues are like eating sugar clouds! They run the gamut of textures. Meringue can be light, soft and silky, chewy or crunchy, even chewy and crunchy. It just depends on how you plan to use it or how long you bake it. A soft meringue straight from the mixer is perfect to ice a cake or top a tart. Bake it in the oven low and slow, and the meringue dries out and become nice and crunchy. Bake a little less time at a slightly higher temperature, and the inside will be chewy and the outside nice and crisp.

Meringues are delicious to eat alone as bite-sized Meringue Kisses (page 179), disks sandwiched with ice cream to make a Vacherin Glacé (page 183) or engulfed in whipped cream and rolled in delicious toppings to form Merveilleux (page 175), which are as marvelous as their name.

Meringue consists of just two ingredients: egg whites and sugar. For meringue to be stable and hold its structure, it needs a ratio of twice the amount of sugar to egg white. Now all it takes is to combine the two!

BASE RECIPE: MERINGUE

There are several methods of whipping up meringue and they all happen to be named after countries. Two of my favorites are French and Italian. French, because of the simplicity: All you do is whip up egg whites and slowly add sugar! And Italian because of the stability and foolproof nature of the result. Sugar is heated to a certain temperature and then poured into whipped egg whites to cook and make them fluffy and voluptuous.

My recipes for both meringue types call for varying amounts of egg whites to suit the quantity of meringue needed in the recipes in this book. The French and Italian methods can be used rather interchangeably except when used to top the Tarte au Citron Meringuée ou Pas! (page 71). For that, as it won't be baked in the oven, it's best to go with the Italian method.

Before you start, here are a couple of top tips to help you every time you whip egg whites: For best results, use fresh egg whites (often boxed whites don't whip up). Cleanly separate the egg whites from the yolks. Any bit of yolk can prevent the whites from whipping up. I like to crack the egg on a flat surface, open up into a small bowl and then fish out the yolk with a clean hand. This is best done when the eggs are cold, but whites whip up best when they are at room temperature.

Make sure your whisk attachment and mixing bowl are squeaky clean. If you haven't used them in a while, then give them a good wash, especially if they are stored on a kitchen counter as fat from cooking can cause the whites to not whip.

THE DIFFERENT TYPES OF PEAKS

Soft Peak

Medium Peak

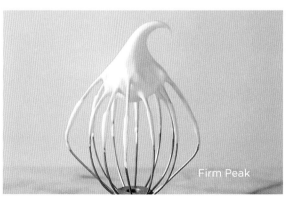

Firm Peak

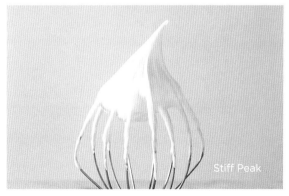

Stiff Peak

BASE RECIPE 1: FRENCH MERINGUE

French meringue is often a part of recipes where lift is needed from the egg whites, such as The Frenchman's Chocolate Mousse (page 123). It's also a good choice for when it will be baked into Meringue Kisses (page 179) or into disks for Merveilleux (page 175) or Vacherin Glacé (page 183).

For French meringue, you'll be adding two types of sugar to the whipped egg whites: granulated sugar and powdered sugar. It can be a bit tricky to have a silky French meringue by using all granulated sugar, so the best approach is to fold in the remaining sugar needed in the form of powdered sugar at the end. Take your time with this one—it can take upwards of ten to fifteen minutes to slowly whip the granulated sugar in. For best results, use super-fine granulated sugar to help it dissolve more easily into the whites.

FRENCH MERINGUE REFERENCE CHART				
Ingredients	Quantities			
Fresh egg whites	2 (~60 g)	3 (~90 g)	4 (~120 g)	6 (~180 g)
Granulated sugar	¼ cup (50 g)	½ cup (100 g)	⅔ cup (130 g)	1 cup (200 g)
Powdered sugar	½ cup (60 g)	¾ cup (90 g)	1 cup (120 g)	1½ cups (180 g)

Preheat your oven to 200°F (90°C).

In the bowl of a stand mixer fitted with the whisk attachment or in a large bowl, using an electric hand mixer, start whipping the egg whites on medium speed until they completely resemble foam (you won't see any liquid egg white on the bottom of the bowl).

Then, increase the speed to medium-high and very slowly add the granulated sugar, about a tablespoon (15 g) at a time, waiting 15 seconds or so between each addition to allow the sugar to incorporate. Add any extracts or food coloring (if called for in the recipe) after you've mixed in all the granulated sugar.

Keep whipping, then check the peak. If it's not at stiff peak, whip for a bit longer and consider increasing the mixer speed. This can take a total of 10 to 15 minutes to do! Look for a very thick meringue. There should be resistance when you move the beater in the meringue. When the beater is lifted, a point should stand straight up.

Sift the powdered sugar over the whipped egg whites in two additions, gently folding in to combine: Use a spatula to go down through the middle and then scrape up the side and over the top. The consistency will become a bit more fluid after folding it. Try to keep as much air as possible in the egg whites.

Continue with piping and baking instructions per the recipe.

BASE RECIPE 2: ITALIAN MERINGUE

This is my personal favorite. I use it as often as I can for its great results every single time. It's fluffy and has a thick sturdy structure, making it perfect to pipe by itself to bake or to smooth over cakes or tarts for a silky luscious touch. As the sugar is heated to a liquid syrup, there's no worry about it not being completely incorporated—also, it means that the final meringue is fully cooked and can be eaten as is right after it's made.

You'll need a thermometer for this one—any old one will do! I prefer a probe as it's more hands-off, only requiring you to keep an eye on the number.

ITALIAN MERINGUE REFERENCE CHART				
Ingredients	Quantities			
Fresh egg whites	2 (~60 g)	3 (~90 g)	4 (~120 g)	6 (~180 g)
Granulated sugar	½ cup + 1 tbsp (115 g)	¾ cup + 2 tbsp (180 g)	1¼ cups (250 g)	1¾ cups (350 g)

If you'll be baking the meringue, preheat your oven to 200°F (90°C).

Pour the granulated sugar into a small saucepan and add enough water to just cover the sugar (this amount varies by the pan size used).

Cook over medium to high heat, watching the temperature. Place the egg whites in the clean bowl of a stand mixer fitted with the whisk attachment. Alternatively, this can be done in a large bowl, using an electric hand mixer.

Once the temperature of the syrup reaches about 215°F (100°C), start whipping the egg whites at medium to high speed. The goal is to have the egg whites at stiff peak when the sugar syrup reaches 238°F (114°C). If the egg whites sit around while the sugar comes to the right temperature, they'll deflate and the meringue won't be as successful. So, keep an eye on both and adjust either the heat or the speed of the mixer to help them both be ready at about the same time.

When the temperature reaches 238°F (114°C), immediately remove the pan from the heat. If your egg whites aren't at stiff peak, increase the mixer speed until they are at that stage (you'll have about 30 seconds for this. Don't stress. It's plenty of time, I promise!). Check by lifting up the beater. The peak should stand straight up.

Reduce the mixer speed to low and slowly pour the hot sugar syrup into the egg whites. Avoid drizzling on the beater; instead, aim for the point in between the whisk and the side of the bowl, pouring down the inside of the bowl.

Increase the mixer speed back to medium-high and whip until the bowl feels just slightly warm to the touch (body temperature). This can take about 5 minutes, or longer, depending on the quantity of egg whites used, so go by the temperature of the bowl.

Whip or fold in any coloring or flavorings at this point (if called for in the recipe).

Continue with piping and baking instructions per the recipe. It's best to use meringue right after it's made, for the smoothest piping.

(CONTINUED)

BAKING NOTES

Work into your baking schedule that meringue needs a long time to bake, then time afterward to cool before using.

Don't open the oven when the meringues are baking, as the temperature change will result in cracks.

It's best for meringues to cool in a turned-off oven. This can take several hours, so I like to make them in the evening and then leave them in the oven overnight. They're sometimes called "Forgotten Cookies" for this reason.

Humidity and meringue are not friends. It doesn't mean you can't bake meringue on a humid day, though! Just make sure the meringue goes into the oven fairly soon after it is made. Also, be sure to leave it to cool for several hours in the oven (or overnight). It will need a longer time to dry out.

TYPES OF PEAKS

To test the peak, lift your beater out of the bowl and turn it to face up. Refer to the photos on page 171.

A soft peak will fall back on itself and not be able to hold its shape.

A medium peak is a bit firmer, but still falls to one side.

A firm peak holds a nice structure, but the top will still fall to the side.

A stiff peak will stand straight up!

FIXES

My meringue cracked: This is from the sudden temperature change of opening the oven or not allowing the meringue to cool long enough in the oven after it's baked.

My meringue has yellow bubbles or is slightly yellow/brown in color: Your oven was too hot. Turn down the temperature by 25 to 50°F (10 to 20°C).

My meringue is hollow/collapses: This usually happens because the speed of the mixer was increased too quickly for a French meringue. Beat at medium until foamy, then increase to high.

My meringues are weeping (liquid is running out): The sugar wasn't completely dissolved in the meringue. Another reason is that it has soaked up too much moisture from the air while being made or while being stored. Usually this happens with a French meringue. The easiest fix is to switch to an Italian meringue.

My meringue is sticky: This means humidity got to it after it was baked (from a rainy day or even a pot of boiling water). Pop them back into a 200°F (90°C) preheated oven for 10 minutes and let cool completely before removing. Et voilà, crisp meringues! Package quickly in airtight containers.

MERVEILLEUX

⁂ MAKES 15 INDIVIDUAL CAKES ⁂

The cakes are a simple base of two things: meringue and whipped cream. I've offered some ideas for how to change them up with flavored whipped cream or a variety of toppings. As is often the case, the most delightful is the most classic: a simple vanilla whipped cream with chocolate shavings on the outside. For the chocolate, I like to shave bars of dark, white and milk chocolate and do a variety of flavors.

The key to these treats is a very firmly whipped cream. It should be whipped to the point of being thick, like buttercream. If whipped less firmly, it will soften the meringues too much. The directions are for individual three- to four-bite merveilleux, but these can be made in any size. To prepare as an 8-inch (20-cm) cake, make two 8-inch (20-cm) circles of meringue before sandwiching them together with whipped cream. The same baking times and assembly instructions remain.

MERINGUE
1 recipe French or Italian Meringue, using 4 egg whites (pages 172 and 173)

TOPPING OPTIONS
About 5 oz (150 g) chocolate of choice (white, dark, milk)—this is between 1 and 2 chocolate bars

Best-quality chocolate sprinkles

About 1 cup (100 g) of whole cookies, such as speculoos, crushed into crumbs

About 1 cup (100 g) finely chopped toasted nuts

WHIPPED CREAM ICING
3 cups (720 ml) heavy cream, cold

¾ cup (90 g) powdered sugar

1 tsp vanilla extract

3 tbsp (45 ml) full-fat mascarpone

Preheat your oven to 200°F (90°C).

PREPARE THE MERINGUE
Make the meringue of your choice.

Dab a little meringue in the corners of your baking sheet and press a piece of parchment paper on top.

Transfer the meringue to a piping bag fitted with a large round tip (10 to 12 mm; see chart, page 12) or cut to a large opening. Make small closed swirls to create thirty 2- to 2½-inch (5- to 6-cm) circles on the prepared baking sheet. You can also simply spoon the meringue onto parchment and smooth with the back of a spoon or knife.

NOTE
To help with piping, trace circles on the parchment paper with a pencil, using the top of a cup or a round cookie cutter. Flip the paper over before starting to pipe. They don't have to be perfect, but you do need two that are the about same size to sandwich together per merveilleux.

(CONTINUED)

Bake for 2 hours. Don't open the oven door while baking. When the timer goes off, turn off the oven, resist the urge to open the door and leave in the oven for at least 1 hour to cool.

PREPARE YOUR TOPPINGS

To shave the chocolate, simply use a vegetable peeler and run it along the edge of the chocolate bar, or process it in a food processor. Place the chocolate and the other toppings in separate large bowls and set aside.

MAKE THE WHIPPED CREAM ICING

In the bowl of a stand mixer fitted with the whisk attachment or in a large bowl, using an electric hand mixer, whip together the cream, powdered sugar, vanilla and mascarpone at medium-high speed until very thick, like a buttercream. The mixture will seem overwhipped. This is beaten more than you would normally whip cream to pipe beautiful swirls on top of a cake. If adding any flavorings (see Notes), add them when the whipped cream is at medium to firm peak. To make two flavors, divide the cream into two bowls at medium peak stage. Then, whip both of them separately to the right state with any flavorings added. Chill.

ASSEMBLE THE MERVEILLEUX

Before starting to ice the meringues, lay out 15 flattened regular-sized cupcake papers to place the cakes on once they're done, or place them directly on a serving platter.

Put a nice tablespoon-sized (15-ml) amount of the cream on top of one of the disks and sandwich another disk on top. Hold between your thumb and first fingers and ice around the sides. Keep a rim of meringue exposed around the bottom so you can easily hold on to it to finish the top.

NOTE

If the meringues aren't stacking nicely because of points or bumps on the cookies, trim them with a paring knife.

Ice the top by mounding the whipped cream on top to make a dome shape.

Smooth with an offset metal spatula or butter knife. Then, roll or sprinkle with toppings and place on a flattened cupcake paper. Chill the bowl of whipped cream as often as you need to throughout the assembly.

Chill the finished merveilleux for about 30 minutes to firm up before serving.

STORAGE

These are best the day they are made, but can last for 1 day in the fridge.

NOTES

Ideas to flavor the cream, added toward the end of whipping:

¼ cup (20 g) unsweetened cocoa powder

1 tbsp (6 g) instant espresso powder

¼ cup (60 g) cookie butter (a spread made from crushed cookies)

MERINGUE KISSES

❧ MAKES 50 ❧

These are just little bites of sugar joy! Treat friends to a fun colorful gift or offer as a little something delicious at a party or fabulous meal. Let your creativity run wild with adding different flavors, toppings and colors! Try cocoa meringues with peppermint bits for holiday gifts or pink meringues with freeze-dried strawberry for a spring wedding shower. Or simply have fun with the food coloring, making them the colors of the rainbow!

1 recipe French or Italian Meringue, using 3 egg whites (pages 172 and 173)

FLAVOR OPTIONS

1 to 2 tsp (2 g) freeze-dried fruit powder (raspberry, strawberry, etc.)

1 to 2 tsp (2 g) instant espresso powder

Lemon, lime, grapefruit or orange zest

¼ tsp extract (vanilla, almond, lemon, peppermint, etc.)

2 to 3 tbsp (10 to 15 g) unsweetened cocoa powder—sifted into the finished meringue and folded in

½ cup (80 g) mini chocolate chips or chocolate pieces, or peppermint pieces, folded into the finished meringue

Preheat your oven to 200°F (90°C) and whip up the meringue of your choice. Adding any color or flavorings at the point indicated in the recipe.

Transfer to a piping bag fitted with a tip of your choice. Dot a little meringue in the corners of your baking sheet and press a piece of parchment paper on top. Pipe little meringue kisses or whatever designs you'd like. Allow for 1 inch (2.5 cm) between each.

Bake for 1½ hours. Don't open the oven door while baking. When the timer goes off, turn off the oven, resist the urge to open the door—and leave in the oven for several hours to cool.

It's a good idea to make these in the evening and let them cool in the oven overnight.

STORAGE

Keep in an airtight container at room temperature for up to 2 weeks.

NOTES

This recipe doubles easily; just make sure you have enough oven space to cook them all at once as it makes a lot (four baking sheets)! Allow lots of time for these to cool in the oven.

One batch can be divided into several different concoctions; just remember to be relatively quick, as the meringue looks best piped right after it's been made.

If adding food coloring, it's recommended to use gel or powdered, as adding liquid to a meringue can cause problems. For a swirl of color, paint a small amount of gel food coloring in a stripe down the inside of your piping bag before filling it with the meringue.

MIXED BERRY MACARON CAKE

✥ SERVES 8 TO 10 ✣

This pretty cake is light and refreshing, and just perfect for a summer day! A large macaron makes up the base. It is piled high with lemon curd mixed with whipped cream and lots and lots of berries. The beauty of doing macaron like this is that there is no pressure in how it looks. The piping doesn't have to be perfect, as it's hidden. Instead, we are celebrating the flavor and the crisp yet slightly chewy texture of the meringue-based batter, which is the beauty of a delicious macaron.

LIGHT LEMON CURD
1 recipe Smaller Batch Lemon Curd (page 67)

1⅓ cups (320 ml) heavy cream

FRENCH MACARON BASE
100 g egg whites (from about 3 large eggs)

100 g (½ cup) granulated sugar

135 g (1⅓ cups) almond flour

120 g (1 cup) powdered sugar

Gel or powdered food coloring (optional)

TO DECORATE
Berry jam of choice to fill the French macaron shells, or use the reserved lemon curd from this recipe

About 3 cups (400 g) mixed fresh berries

"Snow" powdered sugar, to decorate (optional)

BEGIN THE LIGHT LEMON CURD
Prepare the smaller batch of lemon curd, keeping the heavy cream aside, chilled, for use later. The curd will need to chill for at least 1 hour.

MAKE THE FRENCH MACARON BASE
Preheat your oven to 325°F (165°C). If you have convection, this is a great time to use it! The temperature would remain the same; the baking time might be 1 minute less.

Trace a 9-inch (23-cm) circle on a piece of parchment paper with a pencil, using either a round cake pan or a dinner plate as a guide. Flip the paper over and place on a baking sheet for later.

Place the egg whites in the bowl of a stand mixer fitted with the whisk attachment or in a large bowl, using an electric hand mixer, and the granulated sugar in a separate bowl nearby. Sieve together the almond flour and powdered sugar. Set aside.

Make a French meringue: Whisk the egg whites on medium speed. When they are foaming and there is no liquid egg white left in the bowl, increase the speed to medium-high. Gradually add the granulated sugar and whip until the meringue is at stiff peak, adding any food coloring toward the end (use either gel or powdered—liquid can add too much moisture and cause cracks).

Fold in the sifted almond flour mixture in thirds, mixing until the batter falls from the spatula in a thick ribbon. Be careful to not overmix to where the batter is too liquid, as this will often cause the macaron to be flat and not develop a ruffly foot around the edge. After adding the third addition, check for this texture frequently as it's easy to overmix. The batter will become smoother the more you fold and deflate the egg whites until it flows a little like lava in the bowl: When you pick up a big scoop, turn your spatula to the side; the batter should fall slowly in a thick ribbon.

(CONTINUED)

Transfer to a piping bag fitted with a large round tip (10 mm; see chart, page 12). Dot macaron batter in the corners of a baking sheet and press the piece of parchment on the dots to "glue" it down. Starting in the center of the traced circle, pipe a swirl out to the edges to completely fill the area with batter.

Let sit at room temperature for 15 minutes. Then, bake for 18 to 20 minutes. Open the oven door to release the steam several times throughout the baking time.

To see whether the macaron disk is baked, open the oven and gently try to wiggle the top with several fingers. If it doesn't move, it's ready and fully cooked inside. If it moves, bake for another 1 to 2 minutes and test again.

While the large circle is baking, use the leftover batter to pipe individual macarons to decorate the top or enjoy later. Line a baking sheet with parchment or a silicone baking mat. Pipe 1½-inch (4-cm) circles on the parchment or mat. Hit the bottom of the pan several times to release air bubbles. Time it so they will sit out at room temperature for 15 minutes and then be put into the oven after the big macaron disk is done. Bake the small macarons for 12 to 15 minutes, doing the "wiggle" test as noted earlier, to see when they are baked through.

Remove from the oven and let cool completely on the baking sheets before removing from the parchment or silicone mat.

FINISH THE LIGHT LEMON CURD

Let the prepared lemon curd sit on the counter for about 30 minutes to warm slightly. You want the curd to still be cool but warm enough to where it is fluid and easy to stir before folding it with the whipped cream.

Measure out 1 cup (265 g) of lemon curd to make the light lemon curd. Reserve the remaining curd to fill the individual macarons you made or to enjoy later on toast, sandwiched between cookies or to fill a cake. It can also be frozen. Alternatively, the macarons can be sandwiched with jam, if you prefer.

In the bowl of a stand mixer fitted with the whisk attachment or in a large bowl, using an electric hand mixer, whip the heavy cream to medium-firm peak and fold with the lemon curd until smooth. Transfer to a piping bag fitted with a decorative tip of your choice (I used a large round tip [12 mm] in the photo).

Peel the large macaron disk off the parchment paper and place, top side down, on a serving plate. Start by piping around the edges and then working toward the center, completely filling the circle.

Decorate the top with the berries. I start with the largest berries to provide a base and then add the smaller berries to fill in. I also always reserve several cute strawberries with their stems still attached to put on the top.

Keep chilled and just before serving, place a couple of filled macarons on top. To add even more pizzazz, sprinkle the top with what is called "snow sugar," a type of powdered sugar that doesn't dissolve, so it will stay visible.

MAKE AHEAD

The lemon curd can be made up to 1 week in advance. The cake is best eaten within several hours of being assembled. To help it keep a bit longer, brush the bottom of the macaron circle with melted white chocolate to protect it from the moisture in the light lemon curd. Store extra macarons in an airtight container for up to 3 days in the fridge, or freeze them up to a month.

NOTE

It is highly recommended to use a scale to measure the ingredients in the macaron recipe. See French Macaron Tower (page 75) for additional macaron tips.

VACHERIN GLACÉ

❧ SERVES 10 TO 14 ❧

I like to call this recipe Ice-Cream Cake à la Française! It is rather simple, with just three components: ice cream (bien sûr!), meringue and Chantilly cream. Two meringue disks sandwich the ice cream or sorbet of your choice. Then, the whole cake is iced with sweetened whipped cream for the finishing touch!

Vacherin glacé can be made all in one day, but I suggest splitting the preparation into multiple days. I usually make the meringue the night before so it can dry in the oven overnight.

For the ice cream filling, pick your favorites. I typically use three, as I love the look of three different colored stripes. Sorbet is particularly good for vacherin glacé. Its tangy flavor shines through the whipped cream and melds perfectly with the crisp meringue. I'll often pick a yogurt or vanilla ice cream as one of the layers, too, as I like the blend of zing and creamy.

1 recipe French or Italian Meringue using 6 egg whites (pages 172 and 173)

ICE CREAM/SORBET LAYERS

3 pints (1.5 L) ice cream or sorbet of choice (you'll use about 75% of each pint, about 2 cups [300 g] for each layer)

CHANTILLY WHIPPED CREAM

3 cups (720 ml) heavy cream

½ cup (60 g) powdered sugar

1 tsp vanilla extract or vanilla paste

Berries, for garnish

PREPARE THE MERINGUE

Preheat your oven to 200°F (90°C).

Prepare sheets of parchment paper cut to line 2 baking sheets. Use an 8- to 9-inch (20- to 23-cm) cake pan to trace two circles in pencil on the pieces of parchment. Flip them over and place one on each baking sheet.

Make the meringue of your choice. Transfer to a piping bag fitted with a large round tip (12 mm; see chart, page 12) or decorative tip of choice and fill in the two circles with the meringue. Begin in the center and then swirl out to the sides.

With the remaining meringue, pipe separate pieces, such as lines or swirls, to place on the outside and top of the finished cake for decoration. Switch piping tips for this if you'd like, to maybe a star tip.

Bake for 2 hours. Don't open the oven while baking. When the timer goes off, resist the urge to open the door. Turn off the oven and let the meringue cool inside for several hours.

(CONTINUED)

PREPARE THE ICE CREAM/SORBET LAYERS

Place the ice cream or sorbet in the refrigerator with a plate underneath to collect condensation. Let slowly warm up over the course of about an hour.

Line the cake pan you'll be using with plastic wrap. Use two pieces in each direction, with overhang outside the pan so you can easily lift the ice cream out.

Take from the fridge the first ice cream you'll be using and stir to soften it. Spoon the first layer inside and smooth with the back of a spoon or a metal offset spatula. Freeze for 15 to 30 minutes to firm up. Repeat for the next two layers.

If making in advance, place a piece of plastic wrap on top. Freeze until ready to assemble, at least 30 minutes.

ASSEMBLE THE VACHERIN GLACÉ

Remove the baked meringue circles from the parchment paper. Trim, if needed, with a serrated knife to fit to the size of the pan you used to mold the ice cream.

Take the ice cream insert from the freezer and demold. Sometimes you can simply lift up by the plastic wrap and it will come right out. If it is frozen to the pan, dip into hot water for a couple of seconds until the ice cream partially melts and releases. Remove any plastic on top.

Place a round of meringue on top of the ice cream and gently press down. Turn upside down to put on your serving plate. Remove the rest of the plastic wrap and top with the other meringue circle. Freeze for 20 to 30 minutes, or until firm.

MAKE THE CHANTILLY CREAM

In the bowl of a stand mixer fitted with the whisk attachment or with a hand mixer, whip the heavy cream, powdered sugar and vanilla to firm peak (to where you can easily spread it on the outside of the cake).

Coat the entire cake with the Chantilly cream. Use the remaining Chantilly cream to decorate the top with a couple of flourishes however you like! Press the decorative meringue pieces around the sides and on top. I like to crumble them, too!

If garnishing with fresh berries, wait until serving to put these on top so they aren't frozen.

Freeze until ready to devour. The vacherin will need about 30 minutes to warm up before cutting into it.

STORAGE

Keep in the freezer for up to a week.

MAKE AHEAD

Bake the meringue disks/pieces up to 1 week in advance. Keep in an airtight container at room temperature.

Make the ice cream insert up to 2 weeks in advance, keeping well wrapped in the freezer.

ACKNOWLEDGMENTS

To my parents, for their support in my baking ventures. To my mom, for reading through every single one of these recipes, testing quite a few, and providing feedback around the clock. To my dad, for his engineering skills that figured out dimensions and his classic dad humor that kept me going. I'll always remember those runs to the store when I was a young baker to buy butter and flour at a moment's notice!

To François Merlin, my partner in crime, for his French taste buds and candid feedback, for standing by my side and making trips to the store for a dozen sticks of butter and 60 eggs at a time . . . I couldn't have done it without you!

To my sisters, Catherine and Lillibet Wilkinson, for being lifelong taste testers.

To Kate Hill, for mentoring me and first planting the idea of a cookbook.

To Jennifer Stover, who baked macarons and lemon tarts for me at eight months pregnant, and Laura Pahjule—you two are incredible. Thank you for being my cheering squad!

To Joann Pai and her assistant Kate Devine, for their incredible photography and strawberry moving skills.

To Geraldine Blanche for your constant advice and always lending an ear.

To Peanut, my baking sidekick, my little four-pawed sous chef, who was by my side throughout the whole process of putting this book together. I miss you dearly.

To my recipe testers: Reece, David and Madeleine Fitzgerald, Katharine Riedhart, Christina Collins and Vicki Tyler, for all their invaluable feedback.

To Chef Romain Demailly, for all your tips and guidance.

To Rebecca Fofonoff, my editor, and Page Street Publishing for your amazing support and making the publishing side of putting together a cookbook surprisingly easy!

To the Versailles ladies that picked up cake trials in exchange for sticks of butter (I went through A LOT of butter).

To Pascal, my flower guy at the farmers' market, for all the florals in the photos.

And a big thank-you to my followers and students who were unknowingly my test subjects. All of your questions during classes were taken into account in this book. You make me constantly strive to be a better teacher for all of you!

ABOUT THE AUTHOR

Molly Wilkinson, mentioned on the NBC *Today* show as Instagram's answer to Julia Child, is a pastry chef in Versailles, published in the *New York Times, Wall Street Journal*, *Capital Gazette* and *Living France* magazine. Originally from Dallas, Texas, in 2013 she changed careers to follow her passion by moving to Paris and studying pastry at Le Cordon Bleu. After working at pâtisseries in both France and the United States, she now teaches classes online and out of her eighteenth-century apartment just a five minutes' walk from the Versailles Château. Her method is all about making French pastry easy by breaking down recipes and showing you lots of tips and tricks to help any baker achieve extraordinary results.

INDEX